Street by Street

HASTINGS

BATTLE, BEXHILL, RYE

Catsfield, Crowhurst, Fairlight Cove, Guestling Green, Icklesham, Ninfield, St Leonards, Sedlescombe, Westfield, Winchelsea

2nd edition August 2007
© Automobile Association Developments Limited 2007

Original edition printed August 2002

Published by AA Publishing (a trading name of Automobile Association Developments Limited, whose registered office is Fanum House, Basing View, Basingstoke, Hampshire RG21 4EA. Registered number 1878835).

Produced by the Mapping Services Department of The Automobile Association. (A03386)

A CIP Catalogue record for this book is available from the British Library.

Printed by Oriental Press in Dubai

Key to map pages	ii-iii
Key to map symbols	iv-1
Enlarged map pages	2-3
Main map pages	4-45
Index – towns & villages	46
Index – streets	47-52
Index – featured places	52
Acknowledgements	52

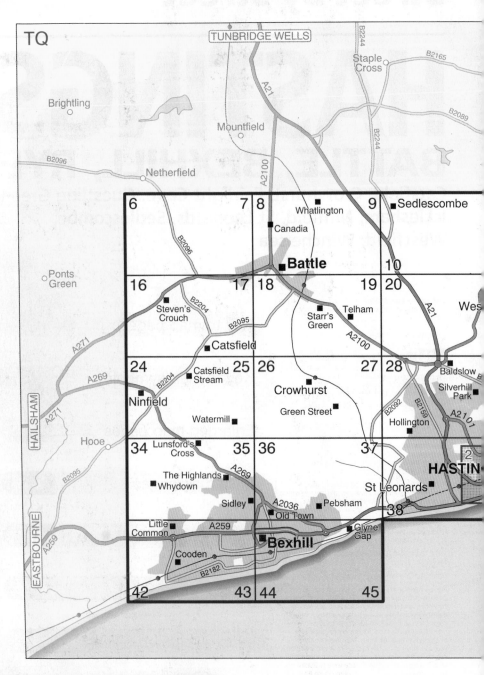

TQ

TUNBRIDGE WELLS

Staple Cross

Brightling

Mountfield

Netherfield

B2096

Ponts Green

| 6 | 7 | 8 | | 9 | Sedlescombe |
Whatlington
Canadia
Battle

10

| 16 | 17 | 18 | 19 | 20 | Wes |
Steven's Crouch
B2204
B2095
Telham
Starr's Green
Catsfield
A2100

| 24 | 25 | 26 | 27 | 28 |
Catsfield Stream
Crowhurst
Green Street
Baldslow
Silverhill Park
Ninfield
Watermill
Hollington
B2092
B2159
A2101

Hooe

| 34 | 35 | 36 | 37 |
Lunsford's Cross
A269
HASTIN
The Highlands
Whydown
St Leonards
Sidley
A2036
Pebsham
38
Old Town

Little Common
A259
Bexhill
Glyne Gap

Cooden
B2182

| 42 | 43 | 44 | 45 |

HAILSHAM

EASTBOURNE

A271

A269

A271

B2095

A259

2

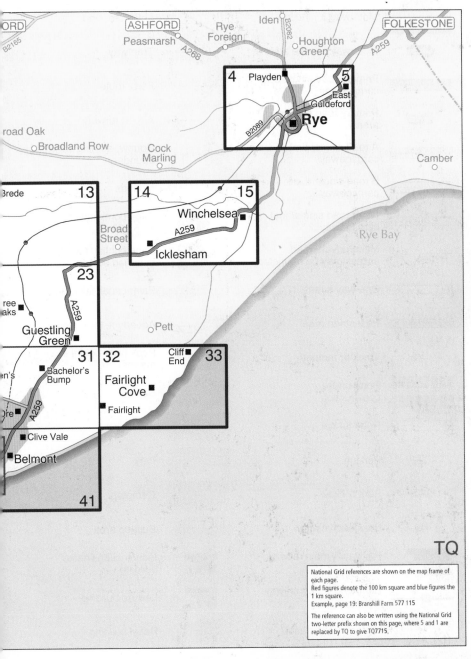

National Grid references are shown on the map frame of each page.
Red figures denote the 100 km square and blue figures the 1 km square.
Example, page 19: Branshill Farm 577 115

The reference can also be written using the National Grid two-letter prefix shown on this page, where 5 and 1 are replaced by TQ to give TQ7715.

4.2 inches to 1 mile   **Scale of main map pages**   **1:15,000**

Junction 9	Motorway & junction
Services	Motorway service area
	Primary road single/dual carriageway
Services	Primary road service area
	A road single/dual carriageway
	B road single/dual carriageway
	Other road single/dual carriageway
	Minor/private road, access may be restricted
←	One-way street
	Pedestrian area
	Track or footpath
	Road under construction
	Road tunnel
P	Parking
P+	Park & Ride
	Bus/coach station
	Railway & main railway station
	Railway & minor railway station
	Underground station
	Light railway & station
+++++++	Preserved private railway

LC	Level crossing
•—•—•—•	Tramway
------	Ferry route
....	Airport runway
— · — · —	County, administrative boundary
ɣɣɣɣɣɣɣɣ	Mounds
17	Page continuation 1:15,000
3	Page continuation to enlarged scale 1:10,000
	River/canal, lake, pier
	Aqueduct, lock, weir
465 ▲ Winter Hill	Peak (with height in metres)
	Beach
	Woodland
	Park
	Cemetery
	Built-up area
	Industrial/business building
	Leisure building
	Retail building
	Other building

⊓⊔⊓⊔⊓⊔	City wall		♜	Castle
A&E	Hospital with 24-hour A&E department		🏛	Historic house or building
PO	Post Office		Wakehurst Place NT	National Trust property
📖	Public library		Ⓜ	Museum or art gallery
i	Tourist Information Centre		🐦	Roman antiquity
_i_	Seasonal Tourist Information Centre		⚱	Ancient site, battlefield or monument
▮▮	Petrol station, 24 hour Major suppliers only		⛏	Industrial interest
✝	Church/chapel		❋	Garden
👥	Public toilets		◉	Garden Centre Garden Centre Association Member
♿	Toilet with disabled facilities		❀	Garden Centre Wyevale Garden Centre
PH	Public house AA recommended		♣	Arboretum
🍴	Restaurant AA inspected		🛒	Farm or animal centre
Madeira Hotel ▬	Hotel AA inspected		🦌	Zoological or wildlife collection
🎭	Theatre or performing arts centre		🦅	Bird collection
🎥	Cinema		🦆	Nature reserve
⚑	Golf course		🐟	Aquarium
▲	Camping AA inspected		**V**	Visitor or heritage centre
🚐	Caravan site AA inspected		♛	Country park
▲🚐	Camping & caravan site AA inspected		⌒	Cave
🎡	Theme park		✗	Windmill
⛪	Abbey, cathedral or priory		🛢	Distillery, brewery or vineyard

Broomgrove

Central Hastings

F **G** **H** 40 **J** **K**

Elphinstone Community School

Parker Road

Firtree Road

Works

Broomgrove

Hurrell

Broomgrove Road

Elphinstone Av 82

Brookland Cl

Beaconsfield Road

Hughenden Road

Works

Ore Station

West Vw

Halton

Halton Crss

Farley

West Vw

Priory

North Terrace

Richmond St

Works

Edga

Mount Pleasant

Road

Calvert Rd

Works

Priory Road

Egremont Pl

Hardwicke Road

Robertsons Hill

All-S CE J

Cromer Walk

Quarry Rd

Quarry Crs

St Mary's Rd

St George's Road

St Thomas's Road

Priory Road

The Glebe

Rotherfield Avenue

OLD LONDON ROAD

Godwin Rd

Tillington Terrace

I

Bexley Infant School

Harold Road

2

Quarry Road

Becker Cl

St Mary's Ter

Emmanuel

Whitefriars Rd

Gladstone Terrace

Priory Road

Castledown CPN Sch

Bembrook Road

Bembrook Rd

Bembrook Road

West Hill Community Centre

Belmont Rd

Belmont Road

Barley Lane

A2101

PO

Nelson Rd

Vicarage Road

Adult Education Centre

Croft Road

Torfield Special School

Harold Road

High

Wickham

3

40

Waterworks Rd

Superstore

P

QUEEN'S ROAD

Stonefield Pl

Pevensey Mews

Milward Road

Milward Crs

Priory Road

Coller Road

Croft Road

West Hill

West Hill

Surgery

Alpine Rd

Gordon Rd

The Croft

Torfield Cl

The Stables Theatre

P

Old Humphrey Avenue

Ebenezers

All Saints Crescent

4

East Hill

1066 Country

Clegg St

St Andrews Market

Stone St

Portland St

Wellington Road

Castledown Av

Castle Hill Rd

Smugglers Adventure

Gloucester Cottages

The Croft

Croft Terrace

Sinnock Square

Surgery

Roebuck St

HIGH STREET

THE BOURNE

All Saints St

Cloudesley Shovell Ho

Strongs Passage

Swaines Passage

Woods Passage

Tackleway

Saxon Shore Way

Old Town

5

Rock-A-Nore Parade

Cem

Castledown Terrace

1066 Story in Hastings Castle

Flower Makers Museum

Old Town Hall Museum of Local History

Plynlimmon Road

Castle Hill

Exmouth Pl

Burdett Pl

Swan

M

Wellesley Ct

Courthope

Oxford Terrace

Winding St

Crown La

East Hill Passage

East Hill Cliff Lift

6

A2101

Indoor Mkt

Wellington Square Medical Cen

St Andrews Market

Wellington Square

Pelham Crs

De Luxe Leisure Cen

Pelham Arcade

West Hill Cliff Lift

West St George St

Mkt street

PO

East St

E-BEACH ST

A259

Net Shops

Fisheries Museum

M

Shipwreck Heritage Centre

Sealife Aquarium

Rock-A-Nore Road

PARK PL

Castle St

Fountain

PELHAM PL

MARINE PDE

EAST-PDE

Amusement Areas

Lifeboat Station

The Stade

7

82

83

09

F **G** **H** 40 **J** **K**

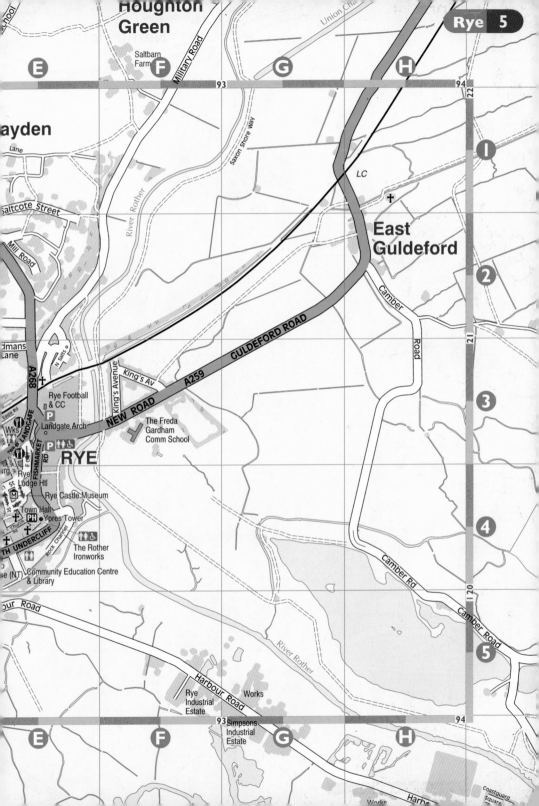

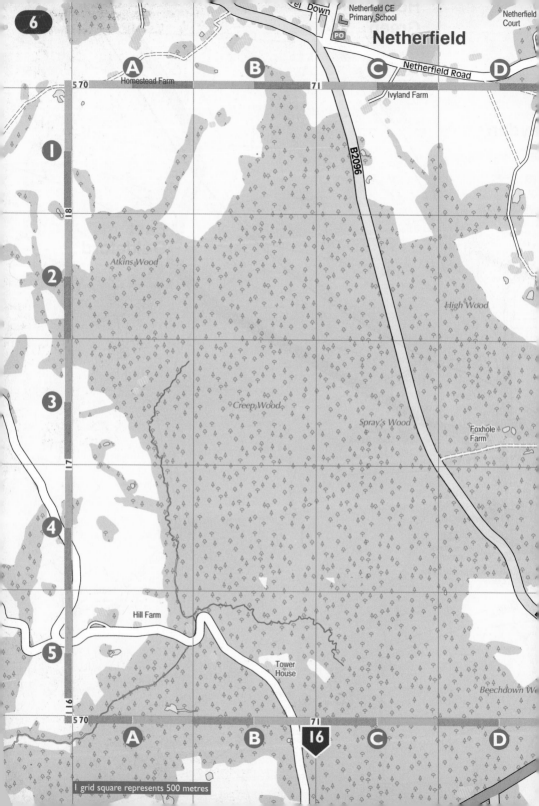

Eatenden Lane

E ✝   F   G   H

Eatenden Wood

73   74

I

Netherfield Road

Burnthouse Wood

18

2 Cana

Le Rette
Farm

Netherfield
Place

Netherfield

Ashes Wood

Hill

Beech

3

8

Kingswell
Farm

17

Nethe

4

Waghurst Lane

Beech
Farm

BA

5

Vale Road

Istlewood

Chain

ROAD

16

73   74

E   F   17   G   TRADE   Battle Gates   H   Asten Flds

A271   NO

Hampden
Close

Battle
CE P

Claverham
Community College

Claverham Close

Claverham Wy

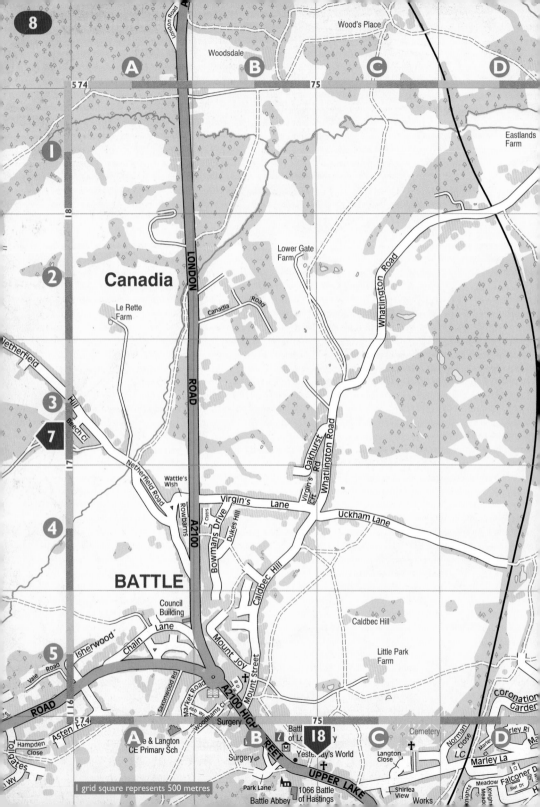

8

A **B** **C** **D**

574 · 75

1 Eastlands Farm

18

2 Canadia
Le Rette Farm · Canadia Road · Lower Gate Farm · Whatlington Road

Netherfield

3 Hill · Beech Cl

7

Netherfield Road · Wattle's Wish · Virgin's Crt · Oakhurst Rd · Whatlington Road

4 Rowbarns · A2100 · Virgin's Lane · Bowmans Drive · Dukes Hill · Uckham Lane

BATTLE

Council Building · Caldbec Hill · Caldbec Hill · Little Park Farm

5 Isherwood Lane · Chain Lane · Mount Joy · Mount Street

Vale Road

ROAD · Saxonwood Rd · Asten Fds · Market Road · Woodhams Cl · A2100 HIGH STREET · Coronation Garden

574 · 75

Cemetery

A ...e & Langton CE Primary Sch · Surgery · Hampden Close

B Battl of Lo... y · Surgery

18

Yester...ay's World · Park Lane · UPPER LAKE · Battle Abbey · 1066 Battle of Hastings

C Langton Close · Shirlea View · Works

D Marley Rd · Marle · Marley La · LC · Meadow Close · Falconer Cl · Knights Meado...

Wood's Place · Woodsdale

I grid square represents 500 metres

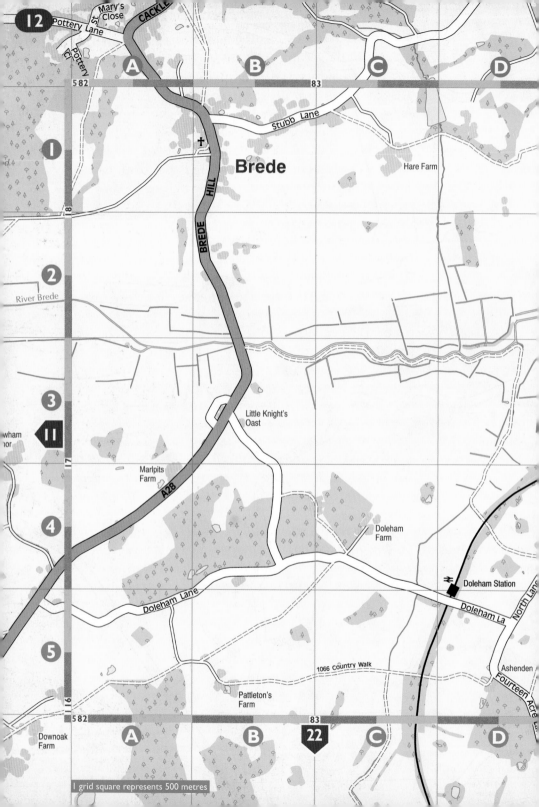

E F G H

Great Park Wood

85 86

Pickdick
Farm

Stonelink
Farm

I

18

River Brede

*Brede
Level*

2

3

17

Lower Snailham

idham
ill

1066 Country Walk

4

North Lane

Stocks
Farm

5

16

85 86

E F **23** G H *Main
Road*

Copshall **Guestling
Thorn**

E F G H

90 91

Winchelsea Station

LC

Station Road

I

Rye Marsh Farm

18

Ferry Bridge

1066 Country Walk

FERRY HILL

TANYARD LANE

F2

L MILITA

North Street

Mill Road

School

Castle St

Barrack Sq

Strand Hill

sea

Road

Winchelsea Court Hall Museum

Hill

Green

Mill

PO

PH

High Street

German St

St Thomas's St

Rookery Lane

Sutton Ind Park

3

Winchelsea

Back Street

ROBERT'S HILL

Kent

St Giles Cl

Saxon Shore Way

TN36

Hogtrough Lane

RECTORY LANE

Friars Road

Winchelsea St Thomas CE Primary School

Greyfriars

4

Crutches Farm

Monks' Walk

Saxon Shore Way

Dimsda

259

1066 Country Walk

Wickham Manor

Jordan Farm

Wickham Rock Lane

1066 Country Walk

116

5

Donald Way

90 91

E F G H

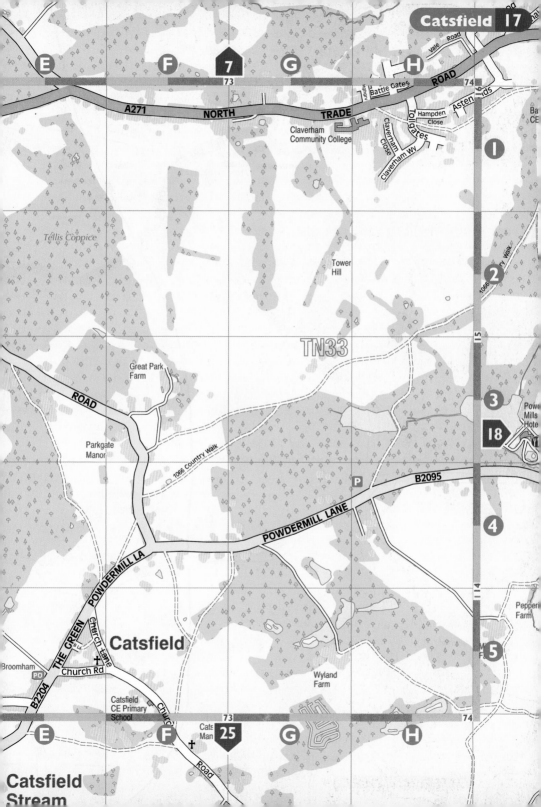

E   F   **7**   G   H

73

Vale Road

A271   NORTH   TRADE   ROAD   74

Battle Gates

High St

Claverham
Community College

Hampden
Close

Toligates

Asten Flds

Claverham Close

Claverham Wy

Ba
CE

I

Téllis Coppice

Tower
Hill

1066 Country Walk

2

15

TN33

ROAD

Great Park
Farm

3

Powe
Mills
Hote

18

Parkgate
Manor

1066 Country Walk

P

B2095

POWDERMILL LANE

4

14

THE GREEN

POWDERMILL LA

Church Lane

B La

Catsfield

Pepperi
Farm

Broomham

PO

B2204

Church Rd

Catsfield
CE Primary
School

Church Road

Wyland
Farm

M
F

5

E   F   Cats Man   **25**   G   H

73   74

**Catsfield
Stream**

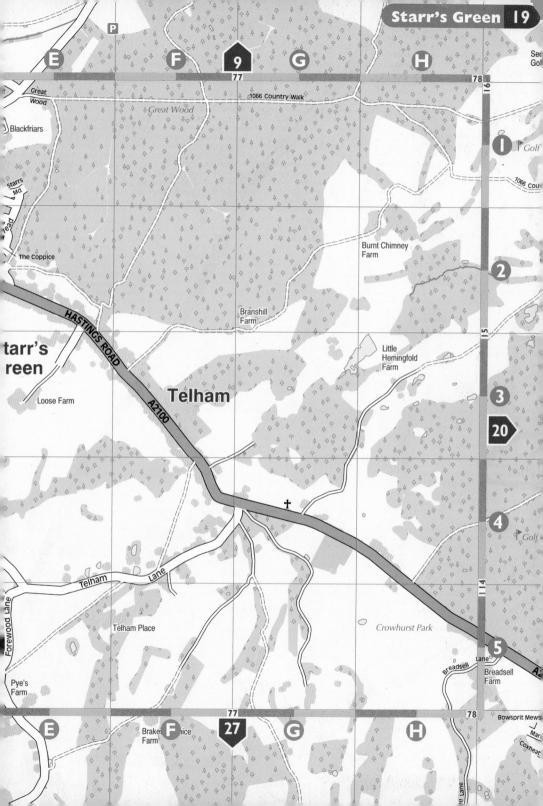

P

E F **9** G H
77

78
16

Great
Wood

1066 Country Walk

Great Wood

Blackfriars

I Golf

Starrs
Md

1066 Cou

The Coppice

Burnt Chimney
Farm

2

HASTINGS ROAD

Branshill
Farm

Little
Hemingfold
Farm

15

tarr's
reen

3

Loose Farm

Telham

20

A2100

†

4

Golf

Telham   Lane

14

Crowhurst Park

Forewood Lane

Telham Place

5

Breadsell
Lane

Breadsell
Farm

Pye's
Farm

A2

Bowsprit Mews

E F **27** G H
77

78

Brakes
Farm

Coxheat

Mar

A B 10 C D
79

578
16

Sedlescombe
Golf Club

Kent Street

Great Buckhurst
Farm

1066 Country Walk

Spray's Lane

1 Golf Course

Norton's
Farm

1066 Country Walk

Kent

Street

Bluemans

Lane

15

2

Ireland's
Farm

A21

Moat Lane

3

19

Stonehouse

4 Golf Course

Stonehouse Drive

Beauport Park

Clarem
School

114

Ebden's Hill

5

Breadsell
Lane

Breadsell
Farm

A2100

BATTLE ROAD

TEN66
Golf Club

Beauport
Park
Hotel

578
Bowsprit Mews

Highwater
View

A Bay Cl B 28 C D
79

Coxheath Cl

Harbour Wy

Stonebeach
Ri

Regent
Place

Brede Cl

Agincourt Cl

A2100 THE RIDGE WEST

Stink
7 Cl

Fletcher A

Creg Cl

Beauport Gdns

A28

JUNCTION
RD

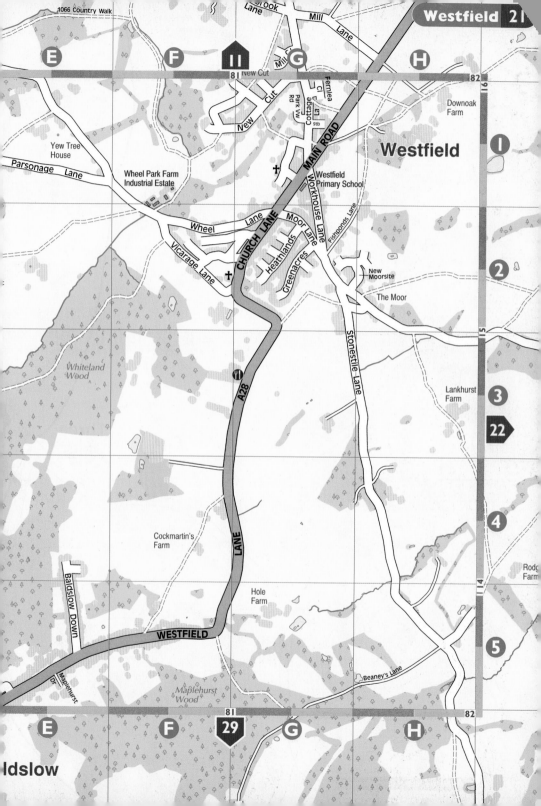

1066 Country Walk

E   F   🏛   G   H

New Cut

New Cut

Mill

Fernlea
Cl

Park VW
Rd

Cottage

Stb

Downoak
Farm

Westfield

I

Yew Tree
House

MAIN ROAD

Westfield
Primary School

Parsonage   Lane

Wheel Park Farm
Industrial Estate

Wheel   Lane

Worknouse Lane

Moor Lane

CHURCH LANE

Fishponds Lane

2

Vicarage Lane

Heathlands

Greenacres

New
Moorsite

The Moor

Whiteland
Wood

🏛

A28

Stonestile Lane

Lankhurst
Farm

3

22

4

Cockmartin's
Farm

LANE

Baldslow Down

Hole
Farm

Rodg
Farm

WESTFIELD

5

Dr

Maplehurst

Beaney's Lane

Maplehurst
Wood

E   F   29   G   H

ldslow

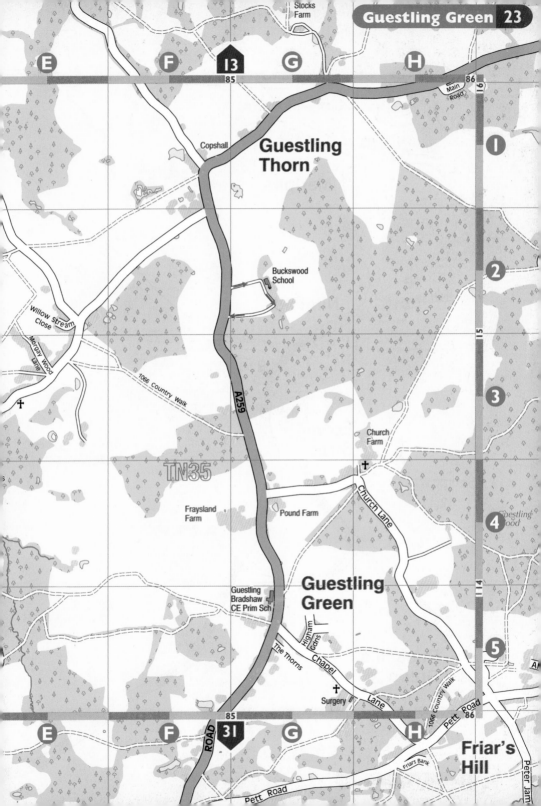

Stocks
Farm

E F **13** G H

85 Main 86
Road 16

Copshall **I**

**Guestling
Thorn**

2

Buckswood
School

15

Willow Stream
Close

3

Morgay Wood
Lane

1066 Country Walk

A259

Church
Farm

✝

TN35

4 Guestling
Wood

Fraysland
Farm

Pound Farm

Church Lane

**Guestling
Green**

14

Guestling
Bradshaw
CE Prim Sch

5

Higham
Gdns

The Thorns

Chapel

A

✝

Surgery

Lane

1066 Country Walk

Pett Road

86

E F **31** G H

85

ROAD

Friars Bank

**Friar's
Hill**

Pett Road

Peter Jam

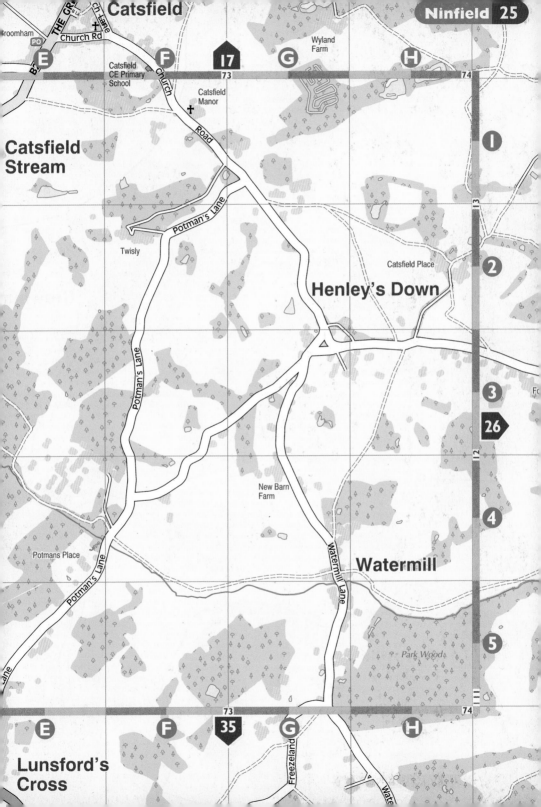

Catsfield

Broomham

PO

Church Rd

Catsfield CE Primary School

Catsfield Manor

Catsfield Stream

Twisly

Potman's Lane

Church Road

Wyland Farm

Catsfield Place

Henley's Down

New Barn Farm

Potmans Place

Potman's Lane

Watermill Lane

Watermill

Park Wood

Lunsford's Cross

Freezeland

E 73 17 G 74 H

I

2

3

26

4

5

E F 35 G H

73 74

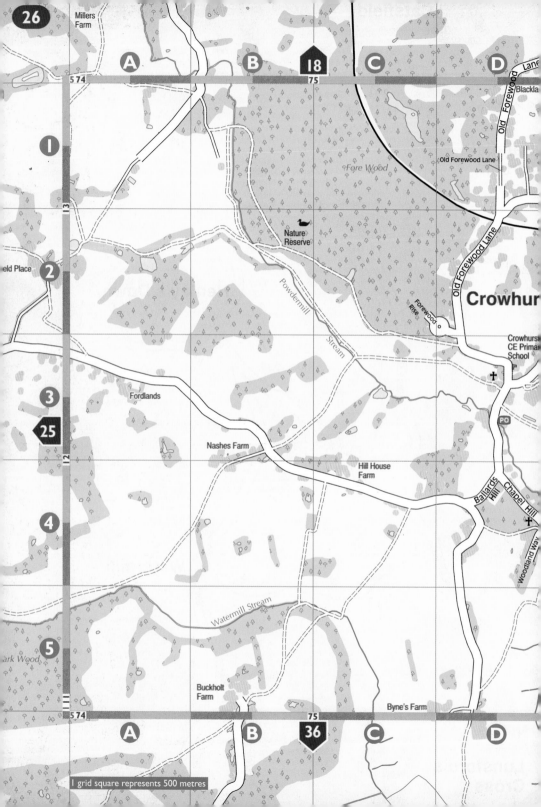

Hollington

1 grid square represents 500 metres

E F 23 G H

High Guns

The thorns

Chapel Lane

Surgery

1066 Country Walk

Pett R8d

Friar's Hill I

Peter James Lane

All.

Friars Bank

Pett Road

Friars Hill

Humphrey's Farm

2

Che Far

Bachelor's Bump

WINCHELSEA ROAD

The Hall

3

Mallydams Wood

32 Hi

Jenner's Lane

Chelsea Lane A259

DAD

illcrest chool

ugh Road

Ditchling Drive

North Seat

Martineau Lane

1066 Country Walk

Battery

Coastguard

Hill

Lane

Fai

ugh

Firle Cl

Beacon Rd

Fairstone Cl

Mill

Fairlight Road

4

The Close

5

The Heights

Tilekiln Lane

Barley Lane

Fairlight Place

Hastings Country Park

E F 41 G H

Fairlight

Covehurst Bay

85 86

32

Allards

Pett Road

A   **B**   **C**   87   **D**

Pett Road

5 86

1066 Country Walk

Friar's Hill

1

Marsham Sewer

Peter James Lane

New Barn Farm

ars Bank

3

Rosemary Lane

2

Cherry Garden Farm

Wakehams Farm

Pett Lev

Stonelynk Farm

Battery Hill

PO

Fairlight Cove

allydams ood

3

Primrose Way

Farley Way

Waites

Clinton Way

31

Hill

Road

Knowle Road

Broad

Way

Waites Lane

Lower

Battery

+

Woodland Way

Stock Dale

The Avenue

Fairlight

Hill

Meadow Way

Blackthorn Way

Smugglers Way

Rockmead Road

4

Coastguard

+

Road

Commanders Walk

Shepherds Way

Bramble Wy

Heather Way

The Close

Warren

Corsethorn Way

Way

Lane

New

Fyrsway

Channel

Road

stings untry rk

5

Fire Hills

Saxon Shore Way

5 86   87

A   **B**   **C**   **D**

1 grid square represents 500 metres

Covehurst

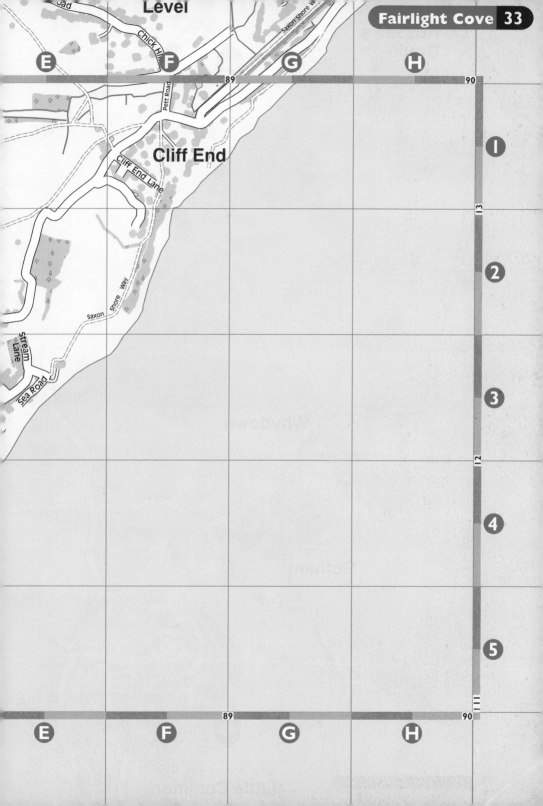

Level

Chick Hill

Saxon Shore W

E

F

G

H

89

90

Pett Road

Cliff End

Cliff End Lane

I

13

2

Saxon Shore Way

Stream Lane

3

12

Sea Road

Wydnow

4

Coltwin

5

11

89

90

E

F

G

H

Little Common

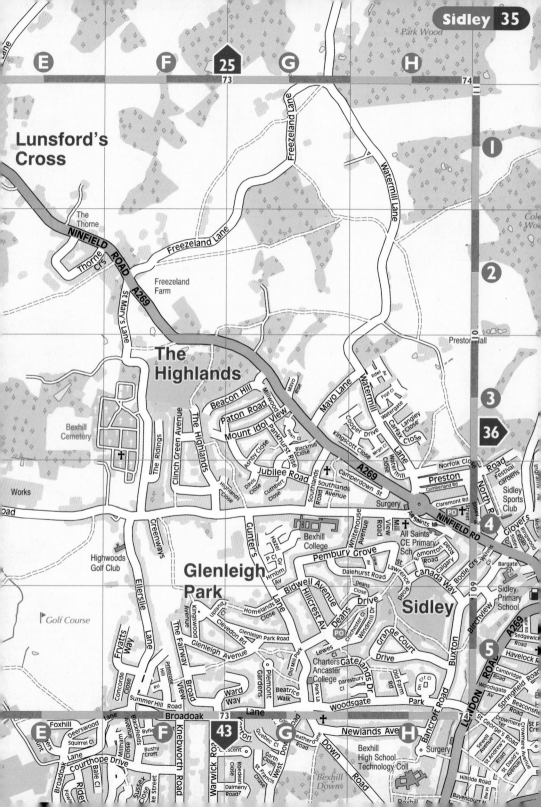

Lower Wilting Farm

Crowhurst Road

Crowhurst R.

E F **27** G H
77

Upper Wilting Farm

Adam's Farm

CROWHURST

Icklesham Dr

Bodiam

Beckley Cl

Pinewood Way

Highfield

Watermill Dr

Church Wood Drive

Community School

ROAD

Water Mint Close

Meadsw'

The Sedges

Field Way

3

38

Reedswood

Asten Close

B2092

4

William Rd

Pebsham Farm

Top Cross Road

Pebsham Drive

Diana Close

Filsham Drive

Pebsham Lane

Pebsham Lane

Bulverhythe

HARLEY SHUTE RD

RD

Conqueror Road

Surgery

Works

BEXHILL Road

5

Silva Cl

Long Avenue

Mistley Close

Road

Cuckfield Close

Wannock Close

Thakeham Close

Dallington Close

Kinver Lane

Singleton Walk

Road

Haven

A259

Bulverhythe

Cliftonville Road

Armbury Mews

Arnside Rd

Martyns

Wyvale Garden Centre

Bridge Way

Glyne

Barn Close

Claxton Road

Alfray Road

Fairlight Close

Hurstwood Close

Wy

F **45** G Works H
77

BEXHILL ROAD

78

ROAD

Pebsham Comm. Prim Sch

School Place

Bexleigh Avenue

Abbey Drive

Hyth Av

Gloucester Av

York Road

Kent Cl

E
78

Glyne

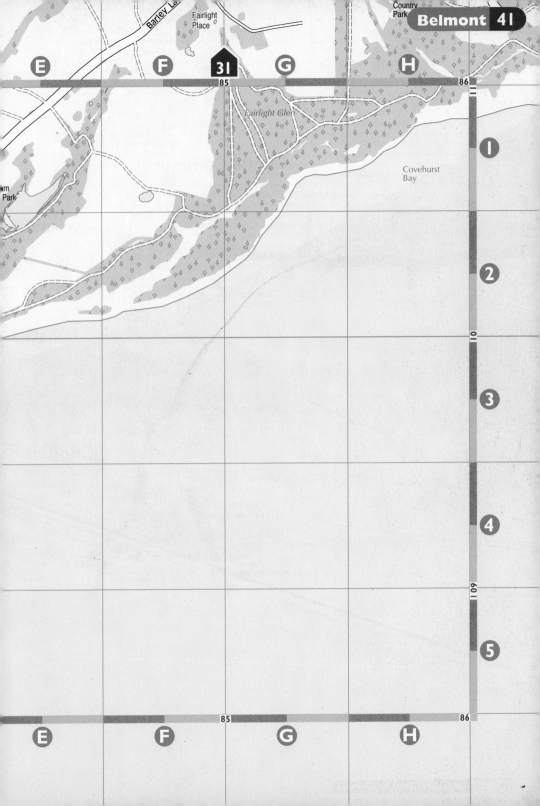

Barley La
Fairlight
Place
Country
Park

E   F   31   G   H

85   86

Fairlight Glen

1

Covehurst
Bay

arn
Park

2

3

4

5

85   86

E   F   G   H

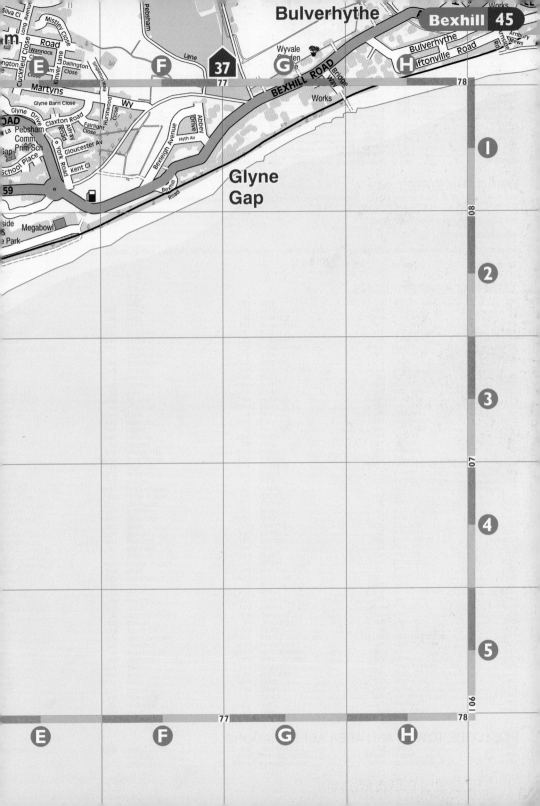

Bulverhythe

Bexhill 45

Wyvale
Garden Centre

Bulverhythe

Cliftonville Road

BEXHILL ROAD

Bridge Way

Works

Martyns

Glyne Barn Close

Glyne Drive

Claxton Road

Allfray Road

Fairlight Close

Gloucester Av

Hyth Av

Abbey Drive

Bexleigh Avenue

York Road

Kent Cl

Pebsham
Comm
Prim Sch

School Place

Glyne
Gap

Bexhill Road

Megabowl

& Park

Road

Pebsham
Lane

Singleton Walk

Cuckfield Close

Long Avenue

Mistley Close

Wannock
Close

Knver Lane

Dallington
Close

Silva Cl

Road

Arnbury
Mews

Works

Arnside
Rd

E F 37 G H

77 78

80

I

2

07

3

4

06

5

E F 77 G 78 H

Bachelor's Bump	31 E2	Crowhurst	26 D2	Icklesham	14 A4	St Leonards	38
Baldslow	28 D1	East Guldeford	5 H2	Lidham Hill	13 E4	Sedlescombe	10
Battle	8 A4	Fairlight	32 A4	Little Common	42 B1	Sidley	35
Belmont	40 C2	Fairlight Cove	32 D3	Lower Street	24 B3	Silverhill	29
Bexhill	43 C2	Friar's Hill	31 H1	Lunsford's Cross	35 E1	Silverhill Park	29
Blacklands	2 B1	Glenleigh Park	35 F4	Maplits	24 B1	Starr's Green	19
Bohemia	39 E3	Glyne Gap	45 C1	Ninfield	24 B2	Steven's Crouch	16
Brede	12 B1	Gotham	34 A4	Old Town	3 K5	Telham	19
Broomgrove	40 A1	Green Street	27 F4	Old Town	36 A5	Three Oaks	22
Bulverhythe	37 C5	Guestling Green	23 C5	Ore	30 C5	Watermill	25
Canadia	8 A2	Guestling Thorn	23 C1	Pebsham	36 D5	Westfield	21
Catsfield	17 F5	Harley Shute	38 B3	Playden	5 E1	West Hill	3
Catsfield Stream	25 E1	Hastings	2 C4	Russell's Green	24 A5	West Marina	38
Cliff End	33 F1	Henley's Down	25 C2	Rye	5 E3	Whatlington	9
Clive Vale	40 D1	The Highlands	35 F3	St Helen's	30 A3	Whydown	34
Cooden	42 D3	Hollington	28 B5	St Helen's Wood	29 G4	Winchelsea	15

USING THE STREET INDEX

Street names are listed alphabetically. Each street name is followed by its postal town or area locality, the Postcode District, the page number, and the reference to the square in which the name is found.

Standard index entries are shown as follows:

Abbey Dr *STLEO* TN38 ....**45** F1

Street names and selected addresses not shown on the map due to scale restrictions are shown in the index with an asterisk:

Ailsworth La *RYE* TN31 * **5** E3

GENERAL ABBREVIATIONS

ACC	ACCESS	E	EAST	LDG	LODGE	R	RIV
ALY	ALLEY	EMB	EMBANKMENT	LGT	LIGHT	RBT	ROUNDABO
AP	APPROACH	EMBY	EMBASSY	LK	LOCK	RD	RO
AR	ARCADE	ESP	ESPLANADE	LKS	LAKES	RDG	RID
ASS	ASSOCIATION	EST	ESTATE	LNDG	LANDING	REP	REPUE
AV	AVENUE	EX	EXCHANGE	LTL	LITTLE	RES	RESERV
BCH	BEACH	EXPY	EXPRESSWAY	LWR	LOWER	RFC	RUGBY FOOTBALL CL
BLDS	BUILDINGS	EXT	EXTENSION	MAG	MAGISTRATE	RI	R
BND	BEND	F/O	FLYOVER	MAN	MANSIONS	RP	RA
BNK	BANK	FC	FOOTBALL CLUB	MD	MEAD	RW	R
BR	BRIDGE	FK	FORK	MDW	MEADOWS	S	SOU
BRK	BROOK	FLD	FIELD	MEM	MEMORIAL	SCH	SCHO
BTM	BOTTOM	FLDS	FIELDS	MI	MILL	SE	SOUTH EA
BUS	BUSINESS	FLS	FALLS	MKT	MARKET	SER	SERVICE AR
BVD	BOULEVARD	FM	FARM	MKTS	MARKETS	SH	SHC
BY	BYPASS	FT	FORT	ML	MALL	SHOP	SHOPP
CATH	CATHEDRAL	FTS	FLATS	MNR	MANOR	SKWY	SKYW
CEM	CEMETERY	FWY	FREEWAY	MS	MEWS	SMT	SUMI
CEN	CENTRE	FY	FERRY	MSN	MISSION	SOC	SOCI
CFT	CROFT	GA	GATE	MT	MOUNT	SP	SP
CH	CHURCH	GAL	GALLERY	MTN	MOUNTAIN	SPR	SPR
CHA	CHASE	GDN	GARDEN	MTS	MOUNTAINS	SQ	SQUA
CHYD	CHURCHYARD	GDNS	GARDENS	MUS	MUSEUM	ST	STR
CIR	CIRCLE	GLD	GLADE	MWY	MOTORWAY	STN	STAT
CIRC	CIRCUS	GLN	GLEN	N	NORTH	STR	STRE
CL	CLOSE	GN	GREEN	NE	NORTH EAST	STRD	STRA
CLFS	CLIFFS	GRA	GROUND	NW	NORTH WEST	SW	SOUTH WI
CMP	CAMP	GRA	GRANGE	O/P	OVERPASS	TDG	TRAD
CNR	CORNER	GRG	GARAGE	OFF	OFFICE	TER	TERRA
CO	COUNTY	GT	GREAT	ORCH	ORCHARD	THWY	THROUGHW
COLL	COLLEGE	GTWY	GATEWAY	OV	OVAL	TNL	TUN
COM	COMMON	GV	GROVE	PAL	PALACE	TOLL	TOLLW
COMM	COMMISSION	HGR	HIGHER	PAS	PASSAGE	TPK	TURNPI
CON	CONVENT	HL	HILL	PAV	PAVILION	TR	TRA
COT	COTTAGE	HLS	HILLS	PDE	PARADE	TRL	TR
COTS	COTTAGES	HO	HOUSE	PH	PUBLIC HOUSE	TWR	TOW
CP	CAPE	HOL	HOLLOW	PK	PARK	U/P	UNDERP
CPS	COPSE	HOSP	HOSPITAL	PKWY	PARKWAY	UNI	UNIVERS
CR	CREEK	HRB	HARBOUR	PL	PLACE	UPR	UPF
CREM	CREMATORIUM	HTH	HEATH	PLN	PLAIN	V	V
CRS	CRESCENT	HTS	HEIGHTS	PLNS	PLAINS	VA	VALI
CSWY	CAUSEWAY	HVN	HAVEN	PLZ	PLAZA	VIAD	VIADU
CT	COURT	HWY	HIGHWAY	POL	POLICE STATION	VIL	VII
CTRL	CENTRAL	IMP	IMPERIAL	PR	PRINCE	VIS	VI
CTS	COURTS	IN	INLET	PREC	PRECINCT	VLG	VILLA
CTYD	COURTYARD	IND EST	INDUSTRIAL ESTATE	PREP	PREPARATORY	VLS	VIL
CUTT	CUTTINGS	INF	INFIRMARY	PRIM	PRIMARY	VW	VI
CV	COVE	INFO	INFORMATION	PROM	PROMENADE	W	W
CYN	CANYON	INT	INTERCHANGE	PRS	PRINCESS	WD	WC
DEPT	DEPARTMENT	IS	ISLAND	PRT	PORT	WHF	WHA
DL	DALE	JCT	JUNCTION	PT	POINT	WK	WA
DM	DAM	JTY	JETTY	PTH	PATH	WKS	WA
DR	DRIVE	KG	KING	PZ	PIAZZA	WLS	WE
DRO	DROVE	KNL	KNOLL	QD	QUADRANT	WY	V
DRY	DRIVEWAY	L	LAKE	QU	QUEEN	YD	YA
DWGS	DWELLINGS	LA	LANE	QY	QUAY	YHA	YOUTH HOS

POSTCODE TOWNS AND AREA ABBREVIATIONS

BAT	Battle	HAS	Hastings	RYE	Rye	WSEA	Winchel
BEX	Bexhill	RBTBR	Robertsbridge	SLVH	Silverhill		
BEXW	Bexhill west	RHAS	Rural Hastings	STLEO	St Leonards		

1

66 Country Wk *BAT* TN33.........19 G1
RHAS TN35.........22 C2
RHAS TN35.........40 E6
WSEA TN36.........15 G1

A

bey Dr *STLEO* TN38.........45 F1
bey Vw *BEX* TN39.........36 B5
bey Wy *BAT* TN33.........8 A5
bots Cl *BAT* TN33.........18 D2
botsfield Cl *HAS* TN34.........29 H5
orn Cl *SLVH* TN37.........29 E4
am Cl *STLEO* TN38.........28 B4
dington Cl *STLEO* TN38.........38 B4
elaide Rd *STLEO* TN38.........28 C5
incourt Cl *SLVH* TN37.........28 B1
sworth La *RYE* TN31 *.........5 E3
oany Man *BEX* TN40 *.........44 A3
oany Rd *BEX* TN40.........44 A3
bany Rd *BEX* TN40.........38 D3
pert Rd *BEX* TN40.........44 A3
HAS TN34.........3 F6
gion La *HAS* TN34 *.........3 G6
bourne Cl *STLEO* TN38.........38 B3
dborough Rd *STLEO* TN37.........39 E2
der Cl *SLVH* TN37.........29 E3
exander Dr *BEXW* TN39.........43 F2
exandra Pde *HAS* TN34.........29 F5
exandra Rd *SLVH* TN37.........39 E2
ford Wy *BEX* TN40.........36 C5
ray Rd *BEX* TN40.........45 E1
red Rd *RHAS* TN35.........30 C5
fred St *STLEO* TN38.........39 E4
riston Cl *BEXW* TN39.........34 C5
en Wy *BEX* TN40.........36 D5
Saints Crs *RHAS* TN35.........3 K4
Saints La *SLVH* TN37.........39 E1
Saints' St *HAS* TN34.........3 J5
na Ct *SLVH* TN37 *.........39 E1
na Ter *SLVH* TN37.........39 E1
na Vls *SLVH* TN37.........39 E1
monry Flds *BAT* TN33 *.........17 H1
ine Rd *HAS* TN34.........3 H4
nanda Cl *BEX* TN40.........36 D4
berstone Cl *HAS* TN34.........30 A4
herst Cl *HAS* TN34.........2 A2
herst Gdns *HAS* TN34.........2 B3
herst Rd *BEX* TN40.........44 A2
HAS TN34.........2 B3
derida St *BEXW* TN39 *.........42 C2
gela Cl *BEX* TN40.........36 D4
glesea Ter *STLEO* TN38.........39 E3
n St *HAS* TN34.........40 B1
trona Cl *BEXW* TN39.........42 C3
vil Pl *BEX* TN40.........29 E5
plewood Cl *SLVH* TN37.........28 D4
ril Pl *BEX* TN40 *.........44 A2
bourvale *STLEO* TN38.........38 C2
chery Rd *STLEO* TN38.........38 D4
chie Ct *STLEO* TN38 *.........38 D5
mstrong Cl *STLEO* TN38.........28 A4
nbury Ms *STLEO* TN38.........38 A5
nside Rd *STLEO* TN38.........38 A5
thur Rd *BEXW* TN39.........43 H2
cot Ms *STLEO* TN38.........38 C3
hbrook Rd *SLVH* TN37.........28 D4
hburnham Rd *RHAS* TN35.........40 C2
hby Cl *BEXW* TN39.........35 G4
hcombe Dr *BEXW* TN39.........42 D3
ndown Cl *STLEO* TN38.........38 A1
ndown Rd *BEX* TN40.........44 C2
henden Av *RYE* TN31.........4 C4
nford Rd *HAS* TN34.........2 C1
nford Wy *HAS* TN34.........39 G1
pen Wy *BEXW* TN39.........42 C2
ten Cl *STLEO* TN38.........38 A4
ten Flds *BAT* TN33.........17 H1
helstan Rd *RHAS* TN35.........40 D1
gustus Wy *SLVH* TN37.........28 B2
sten Wy *RHAS* TN35.........30 D3
e Avenue *RHAS* TN35.........32 D4
ondale Rd *STLEO* TN38.........38 C2

B

ck La *WSEA* TN36.........15 G3
dgers Mt *BEXW* TN39.........43 E1
dgers Wy *SLVH* TN37.........29 F3
ird Dr *HAS* TN34.........29 G5
dslow Down *SLVH* TN37.........21 E4

Baldslow Rd *HAS* TN34.........2 E1
Bale Cl *BEXW* TN39.........43 E1
Bal Edmund *SLVH* TN37 *.........28 D4
Gallards HI *BAT* TN33.........26 D4
Bancroft Rd *BEXW* TN39.........43 H1
Bank Buildings *HAS* TN34 *.........2 E6
Bank Rd *BEXW* TN39.........36 A4
Bargate Cl *BEXW* TN39.........36 A4
Barham Cl *HAS* TN34.........29 G4
Barley Av *RHAS* TN35.........40 C2
Barley La *RHAS* TN35.........40 C2
Barn Cl *SLVH* TN37.........29 E3
Barnfield Cl *HAS* TN34.........2 B4
The Barnhams *BEXW* TN39.........43 E3
Barnhorn Cl *BEXW* TN39.........42 C2
Barnhorn Rd *BEXW* TN39.........42 A2
Barrack Rd *BAT* TN33.........44 A1
Barrack Sq *WSEA* TN36.........15 H3
Barrow HI *SLVH* TN37.........29 E3
Battery HI *RHAS* TN35.........31 H4
Battle Crs *SLVH* TN37.........28 D4
Battle Gates *BAT* TN33.........17 H1
Battle HI *BAT* TN33.........18 C2
Battle Rd *SLVH* TN37.........20 B5
HAS TN34.........28 C3
Bayencourt North *BEXW* TN39.........43 H1
Beachy Head Vw *STLEO* TN38.........28 A1
Beacon HI *BEXW* TN39.........35 F3
Beacon Rd *RHAS* TN35.........31 E4
Beaconsfield Rd *BEX* TN40.........36 A5
HAS TN34.........3 F1
Beaney's La *HAS* TN34.........29 G2
RHAS TN35.........21 H5
Beatrice Wk *BEXW* TN39.........35 G5
Beauchamp Rd *STLEO* TN38.........28 C5
Beaufort Cl *SLVH* TN37.........39 E1
Beaufort Crs *SLVH* TN37.........39 E1
Beaufort Rd *SLVH* TN37.........38 D1
Beauharrow Rd *SLVH* TN37.........28 C2
Beaulieu Gdns *SLVH* TN37.........29 E2
Beaulieu Rd *BEXW* TN39.........42 C4
Beauport Gdns *SLVH* TN37.........28 C1
Beauport Home Farm Cl *SLVH* TN37.........28 C2
Becket Cl *HAS* TN34.........3 C3
Beckley Cl *STLEO* TN38.........37 H1
Bedford Av *BEX* TN40.........44 C3
Bedford Rd *RHAS* TN35.........40 C1
Bedgebury Cl *STLEO* TN38.........38 A1
Beecham Pl *STLEO* TN38.........28 B4
Beech Cl *BAT* TN33.........7 H3
BEXW TN39.........34 C5
Beeching Cl *BEXW* TN39.........43 H2
Beeching Rd *BEXW* TN39.........43 H2
Beechwood Gdns *SLVH* TN37.........29 F3
Belgrave Ct *BEX* TN40 *.........44 B3
Belle HI *BEX* TN40.........44 A1
Bellingham Cl *SLVH* TN37.........28 D4
Belmont Rd *RHAS* TN35.........3 K3
Belvedere Pk *STLEO* TN38.........38 C3
Bembrook Rd *HAS* TN34.........3 J3
Benenden Ri *BEXW* TN39.........29 G5
Berlin Rd *RHAS* TN35.........40 C1
Berwick Cl *BEXW* TN39.........34 C5
Bethune Rd *BEX* TN40.........44 C3
Bethune Wy *HAS* TN34.........3 F3
Beverley Wk *HAS* TN34.........40 A1
Bexhill Rd *BAT* TN33.........24 B4
STLEO TN38.........45 G1
Bexleigh Av *STLEO* TN38.........45 F1
The Bex *BEX* TN40 *.........44 B3
Bicton Gdns *BEXW* TN39.........43 E2
Bidwell Av *BEXW* TN39.........35 G5
Birchington Cl *BEXW* TN39.........42 D2
Birchview *BEXW* TN39.........36 A5
Birch Wy *HAS* TN34.........29 G5
Birk Dl *BEXW* TN39.........42 B2
Birk Hall *BEX* TN40 *.........44 A3
Bishop's Wk *BEX* TN40.........36 D5
Bixlea Pde *BEXW* TN39 *.........42 C2
Blackfields AV *BEXW* TN39.........43 F1
Blacklands Dr *HAS* TN34.........39 H1
Blackman Av *STLEO* TN38.........28 D5
Blackmill Cl *BEXW* TN39.........35 G3
Blacksmiths La *BAT* TN33.........17 E5
Blackthorn Cl *SLVH* TN37.........29 E4
Blackthorn Wy *RHAS* TN35.........32 D4
Blomfield Rd *SLVH* TN37.........39 E3
Bluemans La *BAT* TN33.........20 C2
Bluestone Cl *STLEO* TN38.........38 B1
Bodiam Av *BEX* TN40.........36 B5
Bodiam Dr *STLEO* TN38.........37 H1
Bodle Crs *BEXW* TN39.........35 H4
Bohemia Rd *STLEO* TN38.........38 D2
Bolebrooke Rd *BEX* TN40.........44 B3
The Bordales *BEXW* TN39 *.........38 D2
Boscobel Rd *STLEO* TN38.........38 C4
Boscobel Rd North *STLEO* TN38.........38 C4

The Bourne *HAS* TN34.........3 J5
Bower Cl *SLVH* TN37.........28 D4
Bowmans Dr *BAT* TN33.........8 B4
Bowrey Pl *BEX* TN40.........44 A1
Bowsprit Ms *STLEO* TN38.........28 A1
Boxgrove Cl *BEX* TN40.........44 D2
Boyne Rd *RHAS* TN35.........40 C2
Brackendale *RHAS* TN35.........40 D1
Brackerne Cl *BEXW* TN39.........42 C4
Brading Cl *HAS* TN34.........39 G1
Bramble Wy *RHAS* TN35.........32 D4
Brampton Av *BEXW* TN39.........43 F2
Branksome Rd *STLEO* TN38.........38 C3
Brassey Rd *BEX* TN40.........44 B3
Braybrooke Cl *HAS* TN34.........2 D5
Braybrooke Rd *HAS* TN34.........2 E4
Braybrooke Ter *HAS* TN34.........2 E4
Breadsell La *STLEO* TN38.........27 G3
Brede Cl *SLVH* TN37.........28 B1
Brede HI *RYE* TN31.........12 B1
Brede La *BAT* TN33.........10 B1
Brede Valley Vw *WSEA* TN36.........14 A5
Brendon Rd *HAS* TN34.........30 B5
Brett Dr *BEX* TN40.........44 D2
Briar Cl *RHAS* TN35.........33 E3
The Briary *BEX* TN40.........44 B1
Bridge Wy *STLEO* TN38.........37 G5
Briers Av *SLVH* TN37.........29 E5
Briers Gdns *HAS* TN34.........29 E5
The Briers *SLVH* TN37 *.........29 E4
Brightling Av *RHAS* TN35.........30 D4
Bristol Rd *STLEO* TN38.........28 C5
Brittany Ms *STLEO* TN38.........38 D4
Brittany Rd *STLEO* TN38.........38 D4
Broadlands *RHAS* TN35.........30 D4
Broad Oak Coppice *BEXW* TN39 *.........42 D1
Broadoak La *BEXW* TN39.........43 F1
Broad Vw *BEXW* TN39.........35 F5
The Broadwalk *BEXW* TN39.........42 B2
Broad Wy *RHAS* TN35.........32 D3
The Broadway *RHAS* TN35.........30 D4
Brockley Rd *BEXW* TN39.........43 G3
Brook Cottages *HAS* TN34 *.........3 F4
Brookfield Rd *BEX* TN40.........44 C2
Brookland Cl *HAS* TN34.........3 F1
Brook St *HAS* TN34.........3 F4
Brook Wy *RHAS* TN35.........30 B3
Broomgrove Rd *HAS* TN34.........3 J1
Brunel Rd *STLEO* TN38.........28 A5
Buckholt Av *BEX* TN40.........37 E5
Buckholt La *BEXW* TN39.........36 A2
Buckhurst Rd *BEX* TN40.........44 A2
Buckingham Rd *STLEO* TN38.........28 C4
Bulrush Pl *STLEO* TN38.........38 A1
Bulverhythe Rd *STLEO* TN38.........37 H5
Bunting Cl *STLEO* TN38.........38 A3
Burden Pl *STLEO* TN38.........28 C5
Burdett Pl *HAS* TN34.........3 H5
Burgess Rd *RHAS* TN35.........30 C3
Burhill Wy *STLEO* TN38.........38 B4
Burnside Ms *BEXW* TN39.........43 H2
Burnt Barn Cottages *BAT* TN33 *.........16 C5
Burry Rd *SLVH* TN37.........29 E5
Burton Wy *STLEO* TN38.........38 D5
Burwash Cl *HAS* TN34.........30 A3
Bushy Cft *BEXW* TN39.........43 F1
Butcher's La *RHAS* TN35.........22 C3
Buxton Dr *BEXW* TN39.........35 H5
The Byeway *BEXW* TN39.........42 D1
HAS TN34.........29 H4
Byfields Cft *BEXW* TN39.........43 F1
Byways *SLVH* TN37.........29 F2
Byworth Cl *BEXW* TN39.........34 C5

C

Cadborough Cliff *RYE* TN31.........4 C5
Caldbec HI *BAT* TN33.........8 B5
Calgary Rd *BEXW* TN39.........35 H4
Callums Wk *BEX* TN40.........44 C1
Calvert Rd *HAS* TN34.........3 H1
Camber Cl *BEX* TN40.........36 C5
Camber Rd *RYE* TN31.........5 H5
Cambridge Gdns *HAS* TN34.........2 D6
Cambridge Rd *BEX* TN40.........36 A5
HAS TN34.........2 C6
Camperdown St *BEXW* TN39.........35 G4
Canada Wy *BEXW* TN39.........35 H4
Canadia Rd *BAT* TN33.........8 B2
Cantelupe Ct *BEX* TN40 *.........44 B3
Cantelupe Rd *BEX* TN40.........44 B3
Canterbury Ri *HAS* TN34.........29 G5
Canute Rd *RHAS* TN35.........30 D5
Caple Gdns *STLEO* TN38.........38 D4
Cardiff Rd *STLEO* TN38.........39 E4

Cardinals Cl *BEX* TN40.........36 D5
Carfax Cl *BEXW* TN39.........35 H3
Carinus Gdns *SLVH* TN37.........28 C3
Carisbrooke Rd *STLEO* TN38.........38 D4
Carlisle Pde *HAS* TN34.........2 E7
Carmel Cl *BEXW* TN39.........42 D3
Carpenter Dr *STLEO* TN38.........28 B4
Carvel Ct *STLEO* TN38.........28 A1
Castledown Av *HAS* TN34.........3 G5
Castledown Ter *HAS* TN34.........3 F5
Castle Gdns *HAS* TN34.........3 F6
Castleham Rd *STLEO* TN38.........28 B3
Castle HI *HAS* TN34.........3 G5
Castle Hill Pas *HAS* TN34.........3 F5
Castle Hill Rd *HAS* TN34.........3 F5
Castle St *HAS* TN34.........3 F6
WSEA TN36.........15 H3
Castle View Ms *HAS* TN34 *.........3 F6
Catsfield Cl *STLEO* TN38.........37 H1
Catsfield Rd *BAT* TN33.........16 D2
Cavendish Av *STLEO* TN38.........38 C4
Cavendish Ct *BEX* TN40 *.........44 B3
Caves Rd *STLEO* TN38.........38 C5
Cedar Cl *SLVH* TN37.........29 F3
Celandine Dr *STLEO* TN38.........38 C2
Centurion Ri *HAS* TN34.........30 A4
Ceylon Wk *BEXW* TN39.........43 E3
Chailey Cl *HAS* TN34.........29 G3
Chain La *BAT* TN33.........8 A5
Chalvington Dr *SLVH* TN37 *.........29 E2
Chambers Crs *STLEO* TN38.........28 B5
Chambers Rd *STLEO* TN38.........38 B1
Chanctonbury Dr *HAS* TN34.........29 G2
Chandler Rd *BEXW* TN39.........43 G1
Chandos Ct *BEX* TN40 *.........44 A3
Channel Vw East *BEX* TN40.........44 A3
Channel Vw West *BEX* TN40.........44 A3
Channel Wy *RHAS* TN35.........32 C5
Chantry Av *BEX* TN40.........36 A5
Chantry La *BEX* TN40.........44 A1
Chapel HI *BAT* TN33.........10 A2
BAT TN33.........26 D4
Chapel La *RHAS* TN35.........23 G5
Chapel Park Rd *SLVH* TN37.........39 E3
Chapel Wk *BEX* TN40.........36 C5
Charles Rd *STLEO* TN38.........38 D3
Charles Rd West *STLEO* TN38.........38 D3
Chartres *BEX* TN40.........36 B5
Chartres Ct *BEX* TN40.........36 B5
Chatfield Cl *STLEO* TN38.........28 A4
Chatham Rd *SLVH* TN37 *.........38 D1
Chelgates *BEXW* TN39.........42 C4
Chelsea Cl *BEX* TN40.........44 B2
Chepbourne Rd *BEXW* TN39.........43 H2
Cherry Tree Cl *SLVH* TN37.........39 E3
Cherry Tree Gdns *BEX* TN40.........36 D5
Chestnut Wk *BEXW* TN39.........42 C1
The Cheviots *HAS* TN34.........30 B4
Chichester Cl *BEXW* TN39.........35 H5
Chichester Rd *STLEO* TN38.........38 D1
Chievely Cottages *STLEO* TN38 *.........38 D2
Chiltern Dr *HAS* TN34.........30 B5
Chown's HI *RHAS* TN35.........30 A2
Christine Cl *BEX* TN40.........37 E5
Church Hill Av *BEXW* TN39.........42 D2
Churchill Av *RHAS* TN35.........30 D3
Church in the Wood La *STLEO* TN38.........28 B5
Church La *BAT* TN33.........17 E5
BAT TN33.........24 B3
RHAS TN35.........21 G2
RHAS TN35.........23 H4
Church Pas *HAS* TN34 *.........3 H5
Church Pth *BAT* TN33 *.........24 B3
Church Rd *BAT* TN33.........17 F5
SLVH TN37.........39 E3
Church Sq *RYE* TN31.........5 E4
Church St *BEX* TN40.........44 B1
RHAS TN35.........30 C5
Church Vale Rd *BEX* TN40.........44 B1
Church Wood Dr *STLEO* TN38.........28 B4
Church Wood Wy *STLEO* TN38.........38 B1
Cinque Ports St *RYE* TN31.........4 D4
Cinque Ports Wy *STLEO* TN38.........38 A5
Claremont *HAS* TN34.........2 D6
Claremont Rd *BEXW* TN39.........35 H4
Clarendon Cl *SLVH* TN37.........28 D4
Claverham Cl *BAT* TN33.........17 H1
Claverham Wy *BAT* TN33.........17 H1
Clavering Wk *BEXW* TN39.........42 B4
Claxton Rd *BEX* TN40.........45 E1
Clegg St *HAS* TN34.........3 F4
Clement Hill Rd *HAS* TN34.........30 B5
Clevedon Rd *BEXW* TN39.........35 F5
Cliff End La *RHAS* TN35.........33 F1
Clifford Rd *BEX* TN40.........44 A2
Cliff Wy *RHAS* TN35.........32 D3
Clifton Ri *BEX* TN40.........44 D1

Clifton Rd RHAS TN35.....30 C5
Cliftonville Rd STLEO TN38.....37 H5
Clinch Green Av BEXW TN39.....35 F4
Clinton Crs STLEO TN38.....38 D2
Clinton Wy RHAS TN35.....32 D3
Clive Av RHAS TN35.....40 C1
Clive Vls BAT TN33 *.....18 C2
Clock Tower Ct BEXW TN39 *.....43 H5
The Cloisters BAT TN33.....8 B4
  SLVH TN37.....2 A6
The Close RHAS TN35.....32 A4
  RYE TN31.....4 C3
Cloudesley Rd SLVH TN37.....39 E3
Cloverlea HAS TN34.....29 G3
Clyde Rd STLEO TN38.....39 E4
Coastguard La RHAS TN35.....31 H4
Cobourg Flats HAS TN34 *.....3 H5
Cobourg Pl HAS TN34 *.....3 H5
Cockcrow Wd SLVH TN37.....29 F3
Coghurst Rd RHAS TN35.....30 C4
Colebrooke Rd BEXW TN39.....43 G3
College Rd BEX TN40.....44 C2
Collett Cl STLEO TN38.....28 C3
Collier Rd HAS TN34.....3 H4
Collington Av BEXW TN39.....43 G3
Collington Gv BEXW TN39.....43 G3
Collington La East BEXW TN39.....43 F2
Collington La West BEXW TN39.....42 D3
Collington Park Crs BEXW TN39.....43 F2
Collington Ri BEXW TN39.....43 E2
Collinstone Rd STLEO TN38.....38 C4
Collinswood Dr STLEO TN38.....38 C4
Combermere Rd RHAS TN35.....32 C4
Commanders Wk RHAS TN35.....32 C4
Compton Cl BEX TN40.....44 C2
Concorde Cl STLEO TN38.....35 F5
Conduit Hl RYE TN31.....5 E4
Coneyburrow Gdns
  STLEO TN38.....28 A4
Coneyburrow La BEXW TN39.....42 A1
Conifer Cl HAS TN34.....29 H5
Conqueror Rd STLEO TN38.....38 A4
Conqueror Ter BAT TN33 *.....10 B1
Constable Wy BEX TN40.....44 C1
Conway St STLEO TN38 *.....38 D5
Cooden Cl BEXW TN39.....42 C3
Cooden Dr BEXW TN39.....42 D4
Cooden Ledge STLEO TN38.....28 B1
Cooden Sea Rd BEXW TN39.....42 C4
Cookham Dene BEX TN40.....44 A2
Cookson Gdns HAS TN34.....30 C4
Coombe Shaw BAT TN33.....24 A2
Cooper Dr BEXW TN39.....35 H3
Cooper Ri SLVH TN37.....28 C3
Cooper Rd RYE TN31.....4 C4
Copper Beeches SLVH TN37.....29 E4
The Coppice BAT TN33.....19 E2
  HAS TN34.....2 D3
Copse Cl STLEO TN38.....27 H5
Copse Rd BEXW TN39.....43 E2
Cornfield Ter SLVH TN37.....39 E3
Cornwallis Gdns HAS TN34.....2 E5
Cornwallis St HAS TN34.....2 E5
Cornwallis Ter HAS TN34.....2 D5
Cornwall Rd BEXW TN39.....43 H3
Coronation Gdns BAT TN33.....8 D5
Cotswold Cl HAS TN34.....30 B4
Cottage La BAT TN33.....10 A3
  RHAS TN35.....21 G1
Courthouse Rd BEXW TN39.....43 E1
Courthouse St HAS TN34.....3 H5
The Courtyard HAS TN34 *.....2 C3
Coventry Rd STLEO TN38.....28 C5
Coverdale Av BEXW TN39.....42 C3
The Covert BEXW TN39.....42 C4
Cowdray Cl BEXW TN39.....34 D5
Cowdray Park Rd BEXW TN39.....34 C5
Cowhurst La BEXW TN39.....36 A4
Coxheath Cl STLEO TN38.....28 A1
Craig Cl BAT TN33.....27 E2
Cranbrook Rd SLVH TN37.....39 E2
Cranfield Rd BEX TN40.....44 A2
Cranleigh Cl BEXW TN39.....43 G2
Cranston Av BEXW TN39.....43 F2
Cranston Cl BEXW TN39.....43 F2
Cranston Ri BEXW TN39.....43 F2
Crazy La BAT TN33.....10 A3
Crecy Cl SLVH TN37.....28 B1
The Crescent STLEO TN38.....29 E5
Crofton Park Av BEXW TN39.....43 F3
Croft Rd HAS TN34.....3 J3
Croft Ter HAS TN34.....3 H4
The Croft BEXW TN39 *.....43 G2
  HAS TN34.....3 H4
Cromer Wk HAS TN34.....3 H5
Cross St SLVH TN37.....39 E4
Crossways Man BEX TN40 *.....44 A3
Crouch La BAT TN33.....24 B4
Crowborough Rd RHAS TN35.....30 D4

Crowders La BAT TN33.....16 C2
Crowhurst Rd STLEO TN38.....27 E5
Crowmere Av BEX TN40.....44 A1
Crowmere Ter BEX TN40.....44 A1
Crown La HAS TN34.....3 J5
Cubitt Wy STLEO TN38.....28 A4
Cuckfield Cl BEX TN40.....37 E5
Cumberland Gdns STLEO TN38.....38 D3
Cumberland Rd BEXW TN39.....35 H4
Curlew Ct STLEO TN38.....28 A5
Cuthbert Cl BEXW TN39.....35 G4
Cypress Cl STLEO TN38.....38 C4
Cyprus Pl RYE TN31.....4 D4

D
Dalehurst Rd BEXW TN39.....35 G4
Dallington Cl BEX TN40.....37 E5
Dalmeny Rd BEXW TN39.....43 G1
Dalmore Ct BEXW TN40 *.....44 A3
Dane Court Cl BEXW TN39.....35 H5
Dane Rd STLEO TN38.....38 D3
Daresbury Cl BEXW TN39.....35 G5
Darwell Cl STLEO TN38.....38 A2
Davis Cl BEXW TN39.....35 G4
Deadmans La RYE TN31.....5 E3
Deans Cl BEXW TN39.....35 H4
Deans Dr BEXW TN39.....35 G5
De Cham Av SLVH TN37.....2 A5
De Cham Rd SLVH TN37.....39 E3
De Chardin Dr HAS TN34.....30 A3
Decimus Burton Wy
  STLEO TN38.....39 E4
Deepdene Gdns RHAS TN35.....30 B5
Deerswood La BEXW TN39.....43 F1
Delaware Dr SLVH TN37.....28 B2
De La Warr Ct BEX TN40 *.....44 B3
De La Warr Ms BEX TN40 *.....44 C3
De La Warr Pde BEX TN40.....44 C3
De La Warr Rd BEX TN40.....44 C3
Dell Cl STLEO TN38.....38 C1
De Moleyns Cl BEX TN40.....44 B2
Denehurst Gdns HAS TN34.....30 A3
The Dene RHAS TN35.....30 A3
Denham Cl STLEO TN38.....28 B4
Denmark Pl HAS TN34.....3 F6
Denton Cl RYE TN31.....4 C3
Devonshire Rd BEX TN40.....44 A3
  HAS TN34.....2 E5
Diana Cl BEX TN40.....37 E5
Ditchling Dr RHAS TN35.....31 E4
Dittons Ms STLEO TN38 *.....38 A1
Doleham La RHAS TN35.....12 A5
Dordrecht Wy HAS TN34.....2 C2
Dorset Pl HAS TN34.....2 D6
Dorset Rd BEX TN40.....44 C1
Dorset Rd South BEX TN40.....44 B2
Doucegrove STLEO TN38.....38 C2
Downey Cl SLVH TN37.....28 D2
Downlands Av BEXW TN39.....43 H2
Downlands Cl BEXW TN39.....43 G2
Down Rd BEXW TN39.....43 G1
Downs Rd HAS TN34.....29 H5
Downs Vw BAT TN33.....24 A3
Drapers Wy STLEO TN38.....38 C1
The Drive STLEO TN38.....38 B3
Drury La STLEO TN38.....38 D1
Dudley Rd RHAS TN35.....40 B2
Duke Ms SLVH TN37 *.....38 D1
Duke Rd SLVH TN37.....38 D1
Dukes Hl BAT TN33.....8 B4
Duke St BEXW TN39.....43 F1
  STLEO TN38.....38 D1
Duke Ter SLVH TN37.....38 D1
Dunclutha Rd HAS TN34.....29 H4
Dymond Rd STLEO TN38.....28 C5

E
Eagle Rd RYE TN31.....5 E3
Earl St HAS TN34.....2 E4
East Ascent STLEO TN38.....38 D5
East Beach St HAS TN34.....3 J6
East Cliff RYE TN31.....5 E4
Eastergate BEXW TN39.....42 D1
East Hill Pas HAS TN34.....3 J5
East Pde HAS TN34.....3 H6
East St HAS TN34.....3 H6
  RYE TN31.....5 E4
East View Ter BAT TN33.....10 B1
Eastway BEXW TN39.....42 D1
Eastwood Rd BEXW TN39.....43 G2
Eaton Wk BAT TN33.....9 H1

Ebden's Hl SLVH TN37.....20 D4
Ebenezer Rd HAS TN34.....3 K4
Eden Dr BEXW TN39.....43 D2
Edgar Rd RHAS TN35.....40 C1
Edinburgh Rd BEX TN40.....44 A1
  STLEO TN38.....38 A4
Edith Rd RHAS TN35.....30 C5
Edmonton Rd BEXW TN39.....35 H4
Edmund Rd RHAS TN35.....40 C1
Edward Rd SLVH TN37.....2 A6
Edward Ter STLEO TN38.....28 C4
Edwin Rd RHAS TN35.....40 C1
Effingham Dr BEXW TN39.....42 D3
Egerton Rd BEXW TN39.....43 H3
Egremont Pl HAS TN34.....3 J1
Eight Acre La RHAS TN35.....22 D4
Eisenhower Dr SLVH TN37.....28 B2
Elderwood Cl BEXW TN39.....36 A4
Eldridge Wy SLVH TN37.....29 E2
Elford St HAS TN34.....3 F4
Elim Wk HAS TN34.....39 H1
Elizabeth Rd STLEO TN38.....38 C1
Ellenslea Rd SLVH TN37.....39 E4
Ellerslie La BEXW TN39.....35 F4
Ellis Cl HAS TN34.....2 C6
Elmstead Rd BEX TN40.....44 C1
Elphinstone Av HAS TN34.....3 F1
Elphinstone Gdns HAS TN34.....29 H5
Elphinstone Rd HAS TN34.....3 F1
Elsted Rd BEXW TN39.....42 C4
Elvetham Mt SLVH TN37 *.....39 E4
Emmanuel Rd HAS TN34.....3 H2
Endwell Rd BEX TN40.....44 A3
Ensign Ct STLEO TN38 *.....38 C5
Epsom Cl STLEO TN38.....38 C3
Eridge Cl BEXW TN39.....43 F2
Essenden Rd STLEO TN38.....38 C5
Essex Rd STLEO TN38.....28 C4
Eversfield Pl SLVH TN37.....2 A7
Eversley Cl SLVH TN37.....39 E1
Eversley Rd BEX TN40.....44 A3
  SLVH TN37.....39 E1
Ewhurst Cl HAS TN34.....29 H4
Exmouth Pl HAS TN34.....3 H5

F
Fairfax Av SLVH TN37.....28 B1
Fairfield Cha BEXW TN39.....43 F2
Fairfield Rd SLVH TN37.....29 E2
Fairlight Av RHAS TN35.....30 D5
Fairlight Cl BEX TN40.....45 E1
Fairlight Gdns RHAS TN35.....32 D4
Fairlight Rd RHAS TN35.....30 D5
Fair Meadow RYE TN31.....5 E2
Fairmount Rd BEX TN40.....44 B1
Fairstone Cl RHAS TN35.....31 E4
The Fairway BEXW TN39.....35 F5
  STLEO TN38.....38 B3
Falaise Rd HAS TN34.....2 B6
Falconbury Dr BEXW TN39.....42 D3
Falconer Dr BAT TN33.....18 D1
Farley Bank RHAS TN35.....3 J1
Farley Wy RHAS TN35.....32 C3
Farmlands Cl SLVH TN37.....29 E3
Faygate Cl BEXW TN39.....35 H3
Fearon Rd HAS TN34.....2 E1
Fellows Rd HAS TN34.....30 A5
Fen Ct STLEO TN38.....38 A2
Fernlea Cl RHAS TN35.....21 G1
Fern Rd STLEO TN38.....38 B2
Fernside Av STLEO TN38.....38 B3
Ferring Cl RYE TN31.....4 C3
Ferry Hl WSEA TN36.....15 G2
Ferry Rd RYE TN31.....4 D4
Festival Gdns BEXW TN39.....36 A4
Field Wy STLEO TN38.....38 A3
Filsham Dr BEX TN40.....37 E5
Filsham Rd STLEO TN38.....38 B4
Filsham Va STLEO TN38.....38 B4
The Finches BEX TN40.....44 D2
  STLEO TN38.....28 C3
Findon Cl BEXW TN39.....43 E3
Firle Cl RHAS TN35.....31 E4
Firle Rd BEXW TN39.....42 D2
First Av BEX TN40.....44 D1
The Firs RHAS TN35 *.....40 C2
Fir Tree Cl BEXW TN39.....42 C3
Firtree Rd HAS TN34.....40 A1
Fishmarket Rd RYE TN31.....5 E4
Fishponds La RHAS TN35.....21 G2
Five Houses WSEA TN36 *.....15 G2
Fleet Wood Cl SLVH TN37.....28 D2
Fletcher Av SLVH TN37.....28 B1
Flimwell Cl STLEO TN38.....37 H1
Folkington Gdns SLVH TN37.....29 E3
Fontwell Av BEXW TN39.....42 C1

Ford Rd STLEO TN38.....38
Forest Wy HAS TN34.....
Forewood La BAT TN33.....19
Forewood Ri BAT TN33.....26
Forge Wy SLVH TN37.....29
Fourteen Acre La RHAS TN35.....22
Fowlers Cl BEXW TN39.....43
Foxcote SLVH TN37.....29
Foxhill BEXW TN39.....43
Frant Av BEXW TN39.....42
Frant Cl BEXW TN39.....42
Freckley Hollow BAT TN33.....16
Frederick Rd RHAS TN35.....30
Freezeland La BEXW TN39.....35
Freshwater Av HAS TN34.....29
Frewyn Cl STLEO TN38.....28
Friars Bank RHAS TN35.....31
Friars Hl RHAS TN35.....31
Friars Hill Ter RHAS TN35 *.....31
Friars Rd WSEA TN36.....15
Friar's Wy HAS TN34.....29
Fryatts Wy BEXW TN39.....35
Fulford Cl SLVH TN37.....28
Fulmer Pl BEX TN40 *.....44
Fyning Pl BEXW TN39.....42
Fyrsway RHAS TN35.....32

G
The Gables HAS TN34 *.....29
Gainsborough Rd BEX TN40.....36
Galley Hill Vw BEX TN40.....44
Gammons Wy BAT TN33.....10
Garden Cl BEX TN40.....44
Garden Cottages HAS TN34 *.....2
Gardner Wy STLEO TN38 *.....38
Garth Cl BEXW TN39.....43
Gatehouse Cl BEXW TN39.....42
Gatelands Dr BEXW TN39.....35
Gensing Rd STLEO TN38.....39
Georgian Cl BEX TN40.....44
Georgian Wk STLEO TN38.....38
German St WSEA TN36.....15
Ghyllside Av HAS TN34.....29
Ghyllside Dr HAS TN34.....29
Ghyllside Wy HAS TN34.....29
Gibb Cl BEX TN40.....44
Gilbert Rd STLEO TN38.....38
Gillham Wood Rd BEXW TN39.....42
Gillsman's Dr STLEO TN38.....38
Gillsman's Hl STLEO TN38.....38
Gillsman's Pk STLEO TN38.....38
Githa Rd RHAS TN35.....40
The Glades BEX TN40.....36
Gladstone Rd HAS TN34.....3
Gladstone Ter HAS TN34.....3
Glassenbury Dr BEX TN40.....44
Glebe Cl BEXW TN39.....43
The Glebe HAS TN34.....2
Gleneagles Cl BAT TN33.....18
Gleneagles Dr STLEO TN38.....38
Glengorse BAT TN33.....18
Glenleigh Av BEXW TN39.....43
Glenleigh Park Rd BEXW TN39.....35
Glenthorn Rd BEXW TN39.....43
Glenview Cl RHAS TN35.....40
Gloucester Av BEX TN40.....45
Gloucester Cottages HAS TN34.....3
Glovers La BEXW TN39.....36
Glyndebourne Gdns SLVH TN37.....29
Glynde Cl BEXW TN39 *.....43
Glyne Ascent BEX TN40.....44
Glyne Barn Cl BEX TN40.....45
Glyne Dr BEX TN40.....45
Glyne Hall BEX TN40 *.....45
Godwin Rd RHAS TN35.....40
Goldhurst Gn WSEA TN36.....14
Gordon Rd BAT TN33.....10
Gorselands BAT TN33.....18
The Gorses HAS TN34.....2
Gorsethorn Wy RHAS TN35.....32
The Gorseway BEXW TN39.....42
Grand Av BEX TN40.....
Grand Pde STLEO TN38.....39
Grange Av HAS TN34.....29
Grange Court Dr BEXW TN39.....35
Grange Rd HAS TN34.....29
Graystone La RHAS TN35.....30
Grazebrook Cl BEXW TN39.....42
Great Wd BAT TN33.....19
Greeba Ct STLEO TN38.....38
Greenacres RHAS TN35.....21
Greenfields Cl SLVH TN37.....28
Green La BEXW TN39.....42
The Green BAT TN33.....10
  BAT TN33.....17
  BAT TN33.....24

STLEO TN38 .....38 D2
eenways BEXW TN39 .....35 F4
egory Wk BAT TN33 .....10 A3
enada CI BEXW TN39 .....42 D2
esham Wy STLEO TN38 .....38 C3
esley Rd STLEO TN38 .....28 B3
eville Rd RHAS TN35 .....30 C5
osvenor Crs STLEO TN38 .....38 B5
osvenor Gdns STLEO TN38 .....38 B5
ove Rd RHAS TN35 .....30 D4
e Grove BAT TN33 .....18 D2
BEXW TN39 .....43 E1
RYE TN31 .....5 E4
ldeford Rd RYE TN31 .....5 G3
nter's La BEXW TN39 .....35 G4
rth Rd RHAS TN35 .....40 C2
vyneth Gv BEX TN40 .....36 D4

H

drian Gdns SLVH TN37 .....28 C3
ilsham Ct BEX TN40 * 44 A3
lton Crs HAS TN34 .....3 K1
lton PI HAS TN34 .....3 K1
lton Ter HAS TN34 .....3 K1
milton Gdns RHAS TN35 .....30 D5
milton Ter BEXW TN39 .....43 G2
mpden Ct BAT TN33 .....17 H1
nover CI BEX TN40 .....44 A1
rbour Rd RYE TN31 .....5 E5
rbours Yd BAT TN33 * 18 C1
rbour Wy STLEO TN38 .....28 A1
rdwicke Rd HAS TN34 .....3 K1
re Wy SLVH TN37 .....29 E3
rewood CI BEXW TN39 .....43 G3
rkness Dr HAS TN34 .....30 B3
riequin Gdns SLVH TN37 .....28 C2
rley Shute Rd STLEO TN38 .....37 H5
rley Wy STLEO TN38 .....37 H5
rold Ms STLEO TN38 .....39 E5
rold PI HAS TN34 .....2 E6
rold Rd RHAS TN35 .....3 K3
rrier La BAT TN33 .....18 D1
rrow La SLVH TN37 .....28 D3
rtfield Meadow STLEO TN38 .....2 H5
rtfield Rd BEXW TN39 .....42 D4
rvest Wy SLVH TN37 .....29 E3
rvey CI STLEO TN38 .....28 B4
slam Crs BAT TN33 .....36 D5
stings Rd BAT TN33 .....19 E2
BEX TN40 .....44 B1
therley Rd SLVH TN37 .....39 E4
velock Rd BEX TN40 .....36 A5
HAS TN34 .....2 E5
ven Rd SLVH TN37 .....37 H5
wkhurst Wy BEXW TN39 .....42 A3
wthorn Av RHAS TN35 .....42 D3
wthorn Rd RHAS TN35 .....40 D1
ywood Wy RHAS TN35 .....30 G4
zel Gv BEXW TN39 .....35 G4
zelwood CI BEXW TN39 .....42 B3
zelwood Gdns STLEO TN38 .....29 F3
atherdene Rd BEXW TN39 .....43 G1
ather Wy RHAS TN35 .....32 D4
athfield CI HAS TN34 .....29 H3
athlands RHAS TN35 .....21 G2
ighton CI BEXW TN39 .....42 D3
e Heights RHAS TN35 .....5 J4
lensdene Wk SLVH TN37 * 2 A1
nderson CI HAS TN34 .....29 H5
nley CI RYE TN31 .....4 C3
ron CI STLEO TN38 .....38 A3
rtford CI STLEO TN38 .....28 C4
ver Crs BEXW TN39 .....43 F1
rkman Wy HAS TN34 .....29 F4
sham Gdns RHAS TN35 .....23 G5
gh Bank RHAS TN35 .....40 C1
gh Bank CI RHAS TN35 * 40 C1
gh Beech CI SLVH TN37 .....28 B2
gh Branches BEXW TN39 .....43 E2
ghfield Dr STLEO TN38 .....27 H5
gh Fords CI WSEA TN36 .....14 A5
gh Fords CI WSEA TN36 .....14 A5
ghgrove BAT TN33 .....7 H5
ghlands CI BEXW TN39 .....35 F4
ghlands Gdns STLEO TN38 .....38 D4
ghlands Ms STLEO TN38 * 38 D5
e Highlands BEXW TN39 .....35 F3
ghlea CI SLVH TN37 .....29 E3
gh St BAT TN33 .....8 B5
BAT TN33 .....24 A1
HAS TN34 .....3 J4
RYE TN31 .....5 E4
WSEA TN36 .....15 G3
ghview CI SLVH TN37 .....29 F3
ghwater Vw STLEO TN38 .....3 A1
gh Wickham RHAS TN35 .....3 K3

Highwoods Av BEXW TN39 .....34 C5
Highwoods Ct BEXW TN39 * 43 E1
Hiham Gn WSEA TN36 .....15 C3
Hillborough Ct BEXW TN39 .....42 D2
Hillcrest RYE TN31 .....4 D2
Hillcrest Av BEXW TN39 .....35 C5
Hill Rd RHAS TN35 .....32 A4
Hillside Rd BEX TN40 .....43 H1
HAS TN34 .....29 G5
Hilltop Dr RYE TN31 .....4 D2
Hillyglen CI HAS TN34 .....2 C4
Hoad's Wood Rd HAS TN34 .....29 H5
The Hoe SLVH TN37 .....28 D2
Hogtrough La WSEA TN36 .....15 G3
Hole Farm CI HAS TN34 .....29 G5
Holland Av BEXW TN39 .....42 C2
Hollier's HI BEXW TN39 .....44 A1
Hollinghurst CI SLVH TN37 .....28 D3
Hollinghurst Rd SLVH TN37 .....28 D4
Hollington Ct STLEO TN38 .....38 C3
Hollington Old La STLEO TN38 .....28 D5
Hollington Park CI STLEO TN38 .....38 C2
Hollington Park Rd STLEO TN38 .....38 C2
Hollybank Gdns STLEO TN38 .....38 D2
Holly CI BEXW TN39 .....34 C5
Holmesdale Gdns HAS TN34 .....2 C5
Holmesdale Rd BEXW TN39 .....43 G2
Holmhurst La SLVH TN37 .....28 D2
Holm Oak CI BEXW TN39 .....43 E3
Homelands CI BEXW TN39 .....35 G5
Honeysuckle CI SLVH TN37 .....29 F3
Hoover CI SLVH TN37 .....28 B1
Hopgarden CI HAS TN34 .....2 C4
Hornbeam Av BEXW TN39 .....35 G4
Horntye Pk SLVH TN37 .....2 A5
Horntye Rd SLVH TN37 .....39 E2
Horseshoe CI STLEO TN38 .....38 D3
Howards Crs BEXW TN39 .....42 C2
Howlett CI STLEO TN38 .....28 B4
Hucksteps Rw RYE TN31 * 5 E4
Hughenden PI HAS TN34 .....3 F1
Hughenden Rd HAS TN34 .....3 F1
Hunting CI BEX TN40 .....44 A1
Hurrell Rd HAS TN34 .....40 B1
Hurstwood CI BEX TN40 .....45 F1
Hythe Av STLEO TN38 .....45 F1

I

Ian CI BEX TN40 .....36 D4
Icklesham Dr STLEO TN38 .....27 H5
Ingleside STLEO TN38 .....28 A4
Inglewood Gdns STLEO TN38 .....28 A4
Ingrams Av BEXW TN39 .....36 A4
Insley Ct BEXW TN39 * 43 F3
Ironlatch Av STLEO TN38 .....38 B1
Ironlatch CI STLEO TN38 .....38 B1
Iron Latch Cottages
STLEO TN38 * 38 B1
Isherwood BAT TN33 .....8 A5
Ivyhouse La RHAS TN35 .....30 B3

J

Jacobs Acre BEX TN40 .....44 A1
Jameson Crs STLEO TN38 .....28 C5
Jameson Rd BEX TN40 .....44 B3
Jarretts CI RYE TN31 .....5 E4
Jarvisbrook CI BEXW TN39 .....42 D3
Jenner's La RHAS TN35 .....31 E2
Jevington CI BEXW TN39 .....42 D4
John Macadam Wy SLVH TN37 .....28 C2
Johnson CI SLVH TN37 .....28 B2
Jubilee Rd BEXW TN39 .....35 G4
Junction Rd SLVH TN37 .....28 D1
Juniper CI STLEO TN38 .....28 A5

K

Keats CI STLEO TN38 .....38 B5
Kenilworth Rd STLEO TN38 .....38 D4
Kennedy Rd BEXW TN39 .....44 C2
Kennel La BEXW TN39 .....42 C2
Kensington CI STLEO TN38 .....27 H5
Kent CI BEX TN40 .....45 E1
WSEA TN36 .....15 G3
Kenton CI BEXW TN39 .....43 G1
Kent Rd STLEO TN38 .....38 D5
Kent St BAT TN33 .....20 B1
Kenwood CI HAS TN34 .....39 H1
Keppel Rd HAS TN34 .....30 B1
Kestrel CI BEX TN40 .....44 C2
The Kestrels STLEO TN38 .....28 B3

Kewhurst Av BEXW TN39 .....42 C3
Keymer CI STLEO TN38 .....38 B5
Kildare CI HAS TN34 .....30 B4
Kiln Dr RYE TN31 .....4 D1
King Edward Av HAS TN34 .....29 E5
King Edward CI HAS TN34 .....29 E5
King Offa Wy BEX TN40 .....44 B1
King's Av RYE TN31 .....5 F3
Kings CI BEX TN40 .....44 A2
Kingscott CI SLVH TN37 .....35 G3
Kingsdale CI BAT TN33 .....18 D2
SLVH TN37 .....29 E2
Kingsley CI SLVH TN37 .....28 D3
King's Rd SLVH TN37 .....39 E4
Kingswood Av BEXW TN39 .....35 F5
Kinver La BEX TN40 .....37 E5
Kite CI STLEO TN38 .....38 A3
Knebworth Rd BEXW TN39 .....43 F1
Knights Meadow BAT TN33 .....18 D1
Knole Rd BEX TN40 .....44 B3
Knoll Ri STLEO TN38 .....38 C4
Knowle Av RHAS TN35 .....32 C4
Knowle Rd RHAS TN35 .....32 C3
Knowsley Ct SLVH TN37 .....28 D2

L

Laburnum Gdns BEX TN40 .....36 D5
Lake House CI BEXW TN39 .....42 D2
Lakelands Dr BEXW TN39 .....42 D2
Laleham CI SLVH TN37 .....29 E3
Lancaster Rd STLEO TN38 .....28 B3
Lancing CI HAS TN34 .....29 F5
Landgate RYE TN31 .....5 E3
Landsowne Wy BEX TN40 .....36 C5
Langham CI HAS TN34 .....29 H4
Langham Rd HAS TN34 .....29 H4
Langley CI BEXW TN39 .....35 H3
Langton CI BAT TN33 .....18 C1
Larch CI STLEO TN38 .....38 C2
Larkfield CI STLEO TN38 .....28 A5
Larkhill BEX TN40 .....44 A2
Laton Rd HAS TN34 .....2 E1
Laurel Cottages RHAS TN35 * 4 D1
Laurel La WSEA TN36 .....14 B5
Laurel Wk STLEO TN38 * 28 A5
Lavant CI BEXW TN39 .....34 C5
The Lawn STLEO TN38 .....38 D4
Lea Av RYE TN31 .....4 C3
Leasam La RYE TN31 .....4 C1
Leasingham Gdns BEXW TN39 .....43 G1
The Leas STLEO TN38 * 38 C1
Ledsham Av SLVH TN37 .....28 D3
Ledsham CI SLVH TN37 .....28 D3
Ledsham Pk SLVH TN37 .....28 D3
Ledsham Wy SLVH TN37 .....28 D3
Leeds CI RHAS TN35 .....30 D5
Leopold Flats BEXW TN39 * 43 H2
Leopold Rd BEXW TN39 .....43 H2
Lesley CI BEX TN40 .....36 D4
Lewes CI BEXW TN39 .....35 G5
Lewis Rd STLEO TN38 .....28 C5
Leybourne Gdns SLVH TN37 .....29 E4
Lime CI STLEO TN38 .....38 C2
Lincoln CI STLEO TN38 .....28 B4
Linden Rd BEX TN40 .....44 B1
Links Dr BEX TN40 .....44 C2
The Links BEX TN40 * 44 B3
STLEO TN38 .....38 B3
The Link RYE TN31 .....4 C3
Linley CI BEX TN40 .....44 B2
HAS TN34 .....40 A1
Linley Dr HAS TN34 .....30 A5
Linton Crs HAS TN34 .....2 C4
Linton Rd HAS TN34 .....2 C4
Lionel Rd BEX TN40 .....44 C3
Lion St RYE TN31 .....5 E4
Little Common Rd BEXW TN39 .....42 D2
Little Ridge Av SLVH TN37 .....28 D2
Little Twitten BEXW TN39 .....42 D3
Lodge Rd RHAS TN35 .....40 C2
London Rd BAT TN33 .....8 A2
BEX TN40 .....43 H1
SLVH TN37 .....38 D1
Longacre CI SLVH TN37 .....29 E2
Long Av BEX TN40 .....37 E5
Long La BAT TN33 .....10 A1
Lords La RHAS TN35 .....30 D5
Lovat Md STLEO TN38 .....37 H5
Love La RYE TN31 .....4 D3
Lower Glen Rd SLVH TN37 .....28 D4
Lower Lake BAT TN33 .....18 C1
Lower Park Rd HAS TN34 .....2 C2
Lower South Rd SLVH TN37 .....39 E2
Lower St BAT TN33 .....24 B4
Lower Waites La RHAS TN35 .....32 D4
Loxwood CI BEXW TN39 .....42 C1

Lullington CI BEX TN40 .....37 E5
Lullington Gdns SLVH TN37 .....29 E3
Lychgates CI BEX TN40 .....44 B1
Lyndhurst Av HAS TN34 .....30 A4
Lynwood CI SLVH TN37 .....29 F3
Lytham CI STLEO TN38 .....38 B3

M

Maberley Rd BEXW TN39 .....36 A5
Madeira Dr HAS TN34 .....29 E5
Magdalen Rd BEX TN40 .....44 B2
SLVH TN37 .....2 A6
Magpie CI BEXW TN39 .....34 C5
STLEO TN38 .....38 A3
Main Rd RHAS TN35 .....21 G1
WSEA TN36 .....23 H1
Maitland CI STLEO TN38 .....29 G2
Malvern Wy HAS TN34 .....30 B5
Manchester Rd BAT TN33 .....24 A2
Mann St HAS TN34 .....2 E5
Manor CI WSEA TN36 .....14 B5
Manor Ct BEX TN40 * 44 B1
Manor Rd BEX TN40 .....44 B1
HAS TN34 .....3 G2
Mansell CI BEXW TN39 .....42 C2
Manston Wy HAS TN34 .....2 D1
Maple Av BEXW TN39 .....42 C3
Maple CI BEXW TN39 .....42 C3
Maple Hts SLVH TN37 .....28 D1
Maplehurst CI SLVH TN37 .....28 D1
Maplehurst Dr SLVH TN37 .....21 E5
Maplehurst Ri SLVH TN37 .....28 D1
Maple Wk BEXW TN39 .....42 C3
Marcus Gdns SLVH TN37 .....28 C3
Mare Bay CI STLEO TN38 .....28 A1
Marianne Pk RHAS TN35 .....3 K2
Marina BEX TN40 .....44 A3
Marina Court Av BEX TN40 .....44 A3
Marine Ct STLEO TN38 * 39 E5
Marine Pde HAS TN34 .....3 G6
Market Rd BAT TN33 .....8 A5
RYE TN31 .....4 D4
Market St RYE TN31 .....5 E4
STLEO TN38 .....39 E5
Market Ter STLEO TN38 .....39 E5
Markwick Ter STLEO TN38 .....38 D5
Marlborough CI STLEO TN38 .....38 C2
Marley CI BAT TN33 .....18 D1
Marley Gdns BAT TN33 .....18 D1
Marley La BAT TN33 .....18 D1
Marley Ri BAT TN33 .....18 D1
Marley Rd RYE TN31 .....4 C3
Marline Av STLEO TN38 .....28 C5
Marline Rd STLEO TN38 .....28 C4
Marlow Dr SLVH TN37 .....28 D3
The Marlowes BEX TN40 * 44 B1
Marlpits La BAT TN33 .....24 A1
Martello CI RYE TN31 .....4 D5
Martineau La RHAS TN35 .....31 F3
Martingale CI SLVH TN37 .....29 E3
Martlets BEX TN40 .....44 C1
The Martlets HAS TN34 * 2 D1
Martyns Wy BEX TN40 .....45 E1
Mason Rd RYE TN31 .....4 C4
Maunsell Rd STLEO TN38 .....28 B3
Maxfield La RHAS TN35 .....22 D3
Mayfield La STLEO TN38 .....37 H1
Mayfield Wy BEX TN40 .....44 C1
Mayne Waye HAS TN34 .....30 A4
Mayo La BEXW TN39 .....35 G3
Mayo Ri BEXW TN39 .....35 G3
May Tree Gdns BEX TN40 .....36 D5
Maze HI STLEO TN38 .....38 D4
Maze Hill Ter STLEO TN38 * 38 D4
Meadow CI STLEO TN38 .....28 C4
Meadow Crs BEXW TN39 .....36 A4
Meadow La BAT TN33 .....9 H1
The Meadows SLVH TN37 .....29 E3
Meadowsweet CI STLEO TN38 .....38 A2
Meadow Vw BAT TN33 * 24 B3
Meadow Wy RHAS TN35 .....32 C4
Meads Av BEXW TN39 .....42 C2
Meads CI BEXW TN39 .....42 C2
The Mead BEXW TN39 .....42 D2
Medina Ter STLEO TN38 * 38 C5
Mendip Gdns HAS TN34 .....30 B5
Menzies Rd STLEO TN38 .....38 D1
Mercatoria STLEO TN38 .....39 E5
Mercia Ct BEX TN40 * 44 A1
Mermaid St RYE TN31 .....4 D4
Merrimede CI STLEO TN38 .....38 C4
Mews Rd STLEO TN38 * 38 D5
Michele CI STLEO TN38 .....38 D2
Michelson CI STLEO TN38 .....28 B4
Middle Rd RHAS TN35 .....30 D5
Middlesex Rd BEX TN40 .....44 B3

Middle St *HAS* TN34 .... 2 E5
Mildenhall Dr *SLVH* TN37 .... 28 D4
Milland Cl *BEX* TN40 .... 36 C5
Mill Cl *RHAS* TN35 .... 11 G5
  RHAS TN35 .... 31 E4
Miller's Hl Cottage La *RHAS* TN35.11 G4
Millfield *BAT* TN33 .... 24 A2
Millfield Ri *BEX* TN40 .... 44 A2
Millham Cl *BEXW* TN39 .... 43 F1
Mill La *RHAS* TN35 .... 11 G5
  RHAS TN35 .... 31 E3
Mill Rd *RYE* TN31 .... 5 E2
  WSEA TN36 .... 15 G2
Mill View Rd *BEXW* TN39 .... 35 H4
Millwood Rd *BEXW* TN39 .... 35 G3
Milward Crs *HAS* TN34 .... 3 G4
Milward Rd *HAS* TN34 .... 3 G5
Minsted Sq *BEXW* TN39 .... 42 C4
The Mint *HAS* TN34 .... 4 D4
Mistley Cl *BEX* TN40 .... 37 E5
Mitten Rd *BEX* TN40 .... 44 A2
Moat La *BAT* TN33 .... 20 D3
Monarch Gdns *SLVH* TN37 .... 28 C3
Monks' Wk *WSEA* TN36 .... 15 G4
Monterey Gdns *BEXW* TN39 .... 42 D3
Montgomery Rd *RHAS* TN35 .... 30 D3
Moons Hl *BAT* TN33 .... 24 B2
Moorhen Cl *STLEO* TN38 .... 38 A3
Moorhurst Rd *STLEO* TN38 .... 28 B3
Moor La *RHAS* TN35 .... 21 G2
Morgan Cl *BEXW* TN39 .... 35 H3
Morgay Wood La *RHAS* TN35 .... 23 E3
Morlands Cl *BAT* TN33 .... 24 B3
Moscow Rd *RHAS* TN35 .... 30 C5
Mountbatten Cl *RHAS* TN35 .... 30 D3
Mount Idol Vw *BEXW* TN39 .... 35 G3
Mount Joy *BAT* TN33 .... 8 B5
Mount Pleasant *RHAS* TN35 * 21 G1
  STLEO TN38 * 39 E5
Mount Pleasant Rd *HAS* TN34 .... 3 H1
Mount Rd *RHAS* TN35 .... 40 C1
Mount St *BAT* TN33 .... 8 B5
The Mount *STLEO* TN38 .... 38 D4
Muirfield Ri *STLEO* TN38 .... 38 B4
Mulberry Cl *BEXW* TN39 .... 42 C2
Mulberry Wk *SLVH* TN37 .... 29 F5

N

Napier Rd *STLEO* TN38 .... 28 B4
Nelson Rd *HAS* TN34 .... 3 G3
Netherfield Hl *BAT* TN33 .... 7 H3
Netherfield Rd *BAT* TN33 .... 7 E1
Netherwood Cl *HAS* TN34 .... 29 G3
New Cut *RHAS* TN35 .... 21 G1
New England La *BAT* TN33 .... 10 B4
Newgate Rd *SLVH* TN37 .... 39 E2
Newlands Av *BEXW* TN39 .... 43 C1
Newlands Cl *HAS* TN34 .... 29 G3
Newmans Wy *RHAS* TN35 .... 30 D4
New Moorsite *RHAS* TN35 .... 21 H2
New Park Av *BEX* TN40 .... 44 A2
New Rd *RHAS* TN35 .... 32 B4
  RHAS TN35 .... 40 D1
  RYE TN31 .... 5 F3
Ninfield Rd *BEXW* TN39 .... 35 E2
Nook Cl *RHAS* TN35 .... 30 D5
The Nook *BAT* TN33 * 18 C2
Norfolk Cl *BEXW* TN39 .... 35 H4
Norfolk Dr *STLEO* TN38 .... 28 B4
Norman Cl *BAT* TN33 .... 18 D1
Norman Ct *HAS* TN34 * 2 C7
Normandale *BEXW* TN39 .... 43 F3
Normandy Rd *SLVH* TN37 .... 29 E5
Norman Rd *SLVH* TN37 .... 39 E5
The Normans *BEXW* TN39 * 43 F2
Northampton Wy *STLEO* TN38 .... 28 B4
Northiam Ri *STLEO* TN38 .... 37 H1
North La *RHAS* TN35 .... 12 D5
North Rd *BEXW* TN39 .... 36 A4
  SLVH TN37 .... 39 E2
North Salts *RYE* TN31 .... 5 E3
North St *STLEO* TN38 .... 39 E4
  WSEA TN36 .... 15 G2
North Ter *HAS* TN34 .... 3 K1
North Trade Rd *BAT* TN33 .... 17 F1
Nutley Cl *RYE* TN31 .... 4 C3

O

Oakfield Rd *RHAS* TN35 .... 30 C4
The Oakfield *RYE* TN31 .... 4 D1
Oakfield Wy *RHAS* TN35 .... 34 C5
Oakhurst Cl *HAS* TN34 .... 29 G3
Oakhurst Rd *BAT* TN33 .... 8 C4

Oaklea Cl *SLVH* TN37 .... 29 E4
Oakleigh Rd *BEXW* TN39 .... 42 C2
The Oaks *SLVH* TN37 .... 29 F3
Oak Ter *STLEO* TN38 * 38 D2
Oakwood Av *BEXW* TN39 .... 35 H4
Oakwood Cl *HAS* TN34 .... 29 H5
Oasthouse Cl *SLVH* TN37 .... 29 F3
Oast House Dr *RYE* TN31 .... 4 B5
Oast House Fld *WSEA* TN36 .... 14 B4
Oast House Rd *WSEA* TN36 .... 14 B5
Oban Rd *SLVH* TN37 .... 28 D5
Ochiltree Cl *HAS* TN34 .... 30 A4
Ochiltree Rd *HAS* TN34 .... 30 A4
Ocklynge Cl *BEXW* TN39 .... 42 D1
Ockman La *RYE* TN31 * 5 E4
Offa Ct *BEX* TN40 * 44 A2
Offa Rd *RHAS* TN35 .... 30 C5
Old Church Rd *STLEO* TN38 .... 28 C4
Old Farm Rd *BEX* TN40 .... 44 A1
Old Forewood La *BAT* TN33 .... 26 D2
Old Harrow Rd *SLVH* TN37 .... 28 D4
Old House Gdns *HAS* TN34 .... 29 H4
Old Humphrey Av *HAS* TN34 .... 3 K4
Old London Rd *HAS* TN34 .... 30 C4
  RHAS TN35 .... 3 K2
Old Manor Cl *BEX* TN40 .... 44 B2
Old Mill Pk *BEXW* TN39 .... 35 G5
Old Roar Rd *SLVH* TN37 .... 29 E4
Old Top Rd *RHAS* TN35 .... 30 D4
Oliver Cl *HAS* TN34 .... 2 C6
Orchard Cl *BEX* TN40 * 44 B1
  HAS TN34 .... 39 H1
Orchard Rd *BEX* TN40 .... 36 A5
Orchard Wy *BAT* TN33 .... 10 A1
Ore Pl *HAS* TN34 .... 30 A3
Ormerod Av *STLEO* TN38 .... 28 C4
Osbern Cl *BEXW* TN39 .... 42 C3
Osborne Cl *HAS* TN34 .... 39 G1
Oswald Ct *BEX* TN40 * 44 A2
Oxford Rd *STLEO* TN38 .... 28 C5
Oxford Ter *HAS* TN34 .... 3 J5

P

Pages Av *BEXW* TN39 .... 43 F3
Pages La *BEXW* TN39 .... 43 E3
Pankhurst Cl *BEXW* TN39 .... 35 G3
Pankhurst Ri *BEXW* TN39 .... 35 G3
Park Av *BEXW* TN39 .... 43 H3
  HAS TN34 .... 29 F5
Park Cl *HAS* TN34 .... 29 F5
Park Crs *HAS* TN34 .... 39 F1
Park Dr *HAS* TN34 .... 39 F1
Parker Rd *HAS* TN34 .... 40 A1
Parkhurst Rd *BEX* TN40 .... 44 A3
Park La *BAT* TN33 .... 18 B1
  BEXW TN39 .... 35 C5
Park Lodge Ct *STLEO* TN38 * 38 D4
Park Rd *BEXW* TN39 .... 43 H3
Park Shaw *BAT* TN33 .... 10 A1
Parkstone Rd *HAS* TN34 .... 29 F4
Parks Yd *BAT* TN33 * 18 B1
Park Vw *HAS* TN34 .... 29 F5
Park View Ter *RHAS* TN35 * 21 C1
Park Vw *HAS* TN34 .... 21 C1
Park Wy *HAS* TN34 .... 29 F5
Park Wood Rd *HAS* TN34 .... 29 H2
Parsonage La *RHAS* TN35 .... 21 E1
  WSEA TN36 .... 14 B4
Parsons Cl *HAS* TN34 .... 28 B4
Paton Rd *BEXW* TN39 .... 35 F3
Paxhill Cl *STLEO* TN38 .... 28 A4
Paygate Rd *BAT* TN33 .... 10 A3
Paynton Rd *SLVH* TN37 .... 28 D5
Peartree Fld *WSEA* TN36 .... 14 B4
Peartree La *BEXW* TN39 .... 42 D2
Pebsham Dr *BEX* TN40 .... 37 E5
Pebsham La *BEX* TN40 .... 36 D5
Pegwell Cl *HAS* TN34 .... 2 C1
Pelham Ar *HAS* TN34 .... 3 G6
Pelham Crs *HAS* TN34 .... 3 F6
Pelham Pl *HAS* TN34 .... 3 G6
Pelham St *HAS* TN34 .... 3 F6
Pembury Gv *BEXW* TN39 .... 35 G3
Penhurst Dr *BEX* TN40 .... 36 D5
Penland Rd *BEX* TN40 .... 44 C1
Pennine Ri *HAS* TN34 .... 30 B4
Penny La *BEX* TN40 .... 45 E1
Pentland Cl *SLVH* TN37 .... 29 E3
Percy Rd *RHAS* TN35 .... 30 C5
Perth Rd *SLVH* TN37 .... 28 D5
Peter James La *RHAS* TN35 .... 32 A1
Pett Level Rd *RHAS* TN35 .... 32 D2
Pett Rd *RHAS* TN35 .... 31 H1
  RHAS TN35 .... 33 F1
Pevensey Rd *STLEO* TN38 .... 38 D4
Philip Cole Cl *HAS* TN34 * 3 H5
Picardy *BAT* TN33 .... 18 C1

Pilgrims Wy *HAS* TN34 .... 29 H4
Pilot Rd *HAS* TN34 .... 30 A4
Piltdown Cl *BEXW* TN39 .... 43 H2
  HAS TN34 .... 2 D2
Pinders Rd *RHAS* TN35 .... 40 D1
Pine Av *HAS* TN34 .... 30 B5
Pinehurst Wk *HAS* TN34 .... 30 B5
Pinewoods *BEXW* TN39 .... 43 E2
Pinewood Wy *STLEO* TN38 .... 28 A5
Pipers Cl *BEX* TN40 .... 44 A1
Playden Gdns *HAS* TN34 .... 30 B4
Plemont Gdns *BEXW* TN39 .... 35 G5
Plough La *SLVH* TN37 .... 28 D3
Plover Ct *STLEO* TN38 .... 28 A5
Plumpton Cl *BAT* TN40 .... 36 A5
Plynlimmon Rd *HAS* TN34 .... 3 G2
Ponswood Rd *STLEO* TN38 .... 38 D1
Poplar Cl *BEXW* TN39 .... 35 G4
The Poplars *SLVH* TN37 * 29 E4
Popps La *BEXW* TN39 .... 42 C3
Portfield Cl *BEX* TN40 .... 44 B1
Portland Pl *HAS* TN34 * 3 F5
Portland Ter *HAS* TN34 * 3 F5
Portland Vls *HAS* TN34 * 3 F5
Post Office Pas *HAS* TN34 * 3 H5
Potman's La *BEXW* TN39 .... 35 E1
Pottingfield Rd *RYE* TN31 .... 4 C3
Powdermill La *BAT* TN33 .... 17 E5
Preston Rd *BEXW* TN39 .... 35 H4
Primrose Hl *BEXW* TN39 .... 35 F5
  RHAS TN35 .... 32 D3
Prince's Rd *SLVH* TN37 .... 2 A7
Priory Av *HAS* TN34 .... 2 D3
Priory Cl *HAS* TN34 .... 2 D3
Priory Meadow *HAS* TN34 * 2 E5
Priory Rd *HAS* TN34 .... 3 H4
Priory St *HAS* TN34 .... 2 D3
Prospect Pl *HAS* TN34 .... 2 D6
Prowting Md *BEXW* TN39 .... 42 C2

Q

Quantock Gdns *HAS* TN34 .... 30 B5
Quarry Crs *HAS* TN34 .... 3 G2
Quarry Hl *STLEO* TN38 .... 38 D4
Quarry Rd *HAS* TN34 .... 3 F2
Quebec Cl *BEXW* TN39 .... 43 G1
Quebec Rd *STLEO* TN38 .... 28 C4
Queens Av *HAS* TN34 * 2 E6
Queen's Rd *HAS* TN34 .... 2 E6
Queens Sq *HAS* TN34 .... 2 E6
Queensway *STLEO* TN38 .... 28 A3

R

Radcliffe Cl *HAS* TN34 .... 29 E5
Radnor Ms *STLEO* TN38 * 38 A1
Rafati Wy *BEX* TN40 .... 36 B5
Ranmore Cl *HAS* TN34 .... 29 G3
Raven Ct *BAT* TN33 .... 18 D1
  STLEO TN38 .... 28 A5
Ravens Cl *BEXW* TN39 .... 42 C3
Ravine Cl *HAS* TN34 .... 30 A5
Rectory Cl *STLEO* TN38 .... 38 D2
Rectory La *RYE* TN31 .... 4 D1
  WSEA TN36 .... 15 G4
Rectory Wy *BEX* TN40 .... 44 B1
Redgeland Ri *STLEO* TN38 .... 38 B1
Red Lake Ter *RHAS* TN35 .... 30 D4
Redmayne Dr *HAS* TN34 .... 2 C6
Redwell Av *BEXW* TN39 .... 35 H3
Reedswood Rd *STLEO* TN38 .... 38 A3
Regency Gdns *STLEO* TN38 .... 38 C3
Regent Pl *SLVH* TN37 .... 28 B1
Reginald Rd *BEXW* TN39 .... 43 H2
Renown Cl *BEX* TN40 .... 36 B5
Reynolds Dr *BEX* TN40 .... 44 C1
Richborough Cl *HAS* TN34 .... 29 F4
Richland Cl *RHAS* TN35 .... 30 D4
Richmond Av *BEXW* TN39 .... 43 F3
Richmond Cl *BEXW* TN39 .... 43 G3
Richmond Gv *BEXW* TN39 .... 43 G4
Richmond Rd *BEXW* TN39 .... 43 F3
Richmond St *HAS* TN34 .... 40 C1
Riders Bolt *BEXW* TN39 .... 43 E1
The Ridge *HAS* TN34 .... 30 B4
  SLVH TN37 .... 29 E2
The Ridge West *SLVH* TN37 .... 28 C1
Ridgewood Gdns *BEX* TN40 .... 44 D2
  HAS TN34 .... 29 G3
The Ridings *BEXW* TN39 .... 35 F4
  SLVH TN37 .... 29 E3
Ringwood Rd *BEXW* TN39 .... 36 A4
Robert's Hl *WSEA* TN36 .... 15 G3
Robertson Pas *HAS* TN34 .... 2 D6

Robertsons Hl *RHAS* TN35 .... 3 H
Robertson St *HAS* TN34 2
Robertson Ter *HAS* TN34 2
Robert Tressell Cl *HAS* TN34 2
Robin Hl *BEXW* TN39 42
Robin Ms *SLVH* TN37 * 39
Robsack Av *STLEO* TN38 38
Rochester Rd *SLVH* TN37 38
Rock-a-Nore Pde *HAS* TN34 3
Rock-a-Nore Rd *HAS* TN34 3
Rock Channel *RYE* TN31 5
Rock Cl *RHAS* TN35 30
Rocklands La *RHAS* TN35 40
Rock La *RHAS* TN35 22
Rockmead Rd *RHAS* TN35 32
Roebuck St *HAS* TN34 3
Roedean Cl *BEXW* TN39 43
Rookery La *WSEA* TN36 15
Rookhurst Rd *BEX* TN40 44
Rope Wk *RYE* TN31 5
Roselands *BEXW* TN39 35
Rosemary La *RHAS* TN35 32
Rotherfield Av *BEX* TN40 44
  HAS TN34 3
Rothsay Rd *STLEO* TN38 39
Roundacres Wy *BEX* TN40 36
The Roundel *SLVH* TN37 29
Roundwood Rd *SLVH* TN37 28
Rowan Cl *SLVH* TN37 29
Rowan Gdns *BEX* TN40 36
Rowbarns *BAT* TN33 8
Royal Ms *STLEO* TN38 * 38
Royal Ter *SLVH* TN37 * 39
Royston Gdns *BEX* TN40 44
Rue De Bayeux *BAT* TN33 2
Rushmere Ri *STLEO* TN38 38
Russell St *HAS* TN34 3
Rye Rd *RHAS* TN35 30
Rymill Rd *STLEO* TN38 28

S

Sackville Ms *BEX* TN40 * 44
Sackville Rd *BEXW* TN39 43
The Sackville *BEX* TN40 * 44
St Andrew's Rd *BEX* TN40 44
St Andrew's Sq *HAS* TN34 3
St Andrews Vls *HAS* TN34 * 3
St Anne's Cl *BEX* TN40 44
St Augustine's Cl *BEXW* TN39 43
St Catherine's Cl *SLVH* TN37 2
St Clements Pl *STLEO* TN38 * 39
St David's Av *BEX* TN40 44
St Dominic Cl *STLEO* TN38 38
St Francis Cha *BEXW* TN39 43
St George's Rd *BEX* TN40 44
  HAS TN34 3
St Giles *WSEA* TN36 15
St Helen's Av *HAS* TN34 29
St Helen's Crs *HAS* TN34 2
St Helen's Down *HAS* TN34 30
St Helen's Park Rd *HAS* TN34 2
  HAS TN34 2
St Helen's Rd *HAS* TN34 39
St Helens's Wood Rd *HAS* TN34 29
St James' Av *BEX* TN40 36
St James' Crs *BEX* TN40 36
St James' Rd *BEX* TN40 36
St James's Rd *HAS* TN34 3
St John's Rd *BEX* TN40 36
  SLVH TN37 3
St Kitts *BEXW* TN39 * 43
St Lawrence Rd *BEXW* TN39 35
St Leonards Rd *BEX* TN40 44
St Lucia *BEXW* TN39 * 43
St Margaret's Rd *SLVH* TN37 3
St Margarets Ter *RYE* TN31 4
  SLVH TN37 3
St Marks Cl *BEXW* TN39 42
St Marys Cl *SLVH* TN37 * 3
St Marys Gdns *BAT* TN33 * 18
St Mary's La *BEXW* TN39 3
St Mary's Rd *HAS* TN34 3
St Mary's Ter *HAS* TN34 3
St Matthew's Gdns *STLEO* TN38 38
St Matthew's Rd *STLEO* TN38 38
St Michael's Pl *HAS* TN34 2
St Patrick's Crs *BEX* TN40 44
St Paul's Pl *SLVH* TN37 2
St Paul's Rd *SLVH* TN37 39
St Peters Ct *BEX* TN40 * 44
St Peter's Crs *BEX* TN40 44
St Peter's Rd *SLVH* TN37 3
St Saviour's Rd *STLEO* TN38 38
St Thomas *BEXW* TN39 * 3
St Thomas's Rd *HAS* TN34 3
St Thomas's St *WSEA* TN36 15

'incents SLVH TN37 * 28 D4
'incents Rd STLEO TN38 ......38 B4
cey Cl STLEO TN38 ......38 A1
ehurst Gdns STLEO TN38 ......37 H1
sbury Rd BEX TN40 ......43 H1
LVH TN37 ......39 E2
tcote St RYE TN31 ......5 E1
tdean Cl BEXW TN39 ......43 E3
tdean Wy BEXW TN39 ......42 D3
vington Crs BEXW TN39 ......43 F2
dhurst Gdns HAS TN34 ......29 H2
dhurst Rd RHAS TN35 ......42 A2
down Rd RHAS TN35 ......30 C5
down Wy BEX TN40 ......36 C5
dringham Ct BEX TN40 * 44 B3
dringham Hts STLEO TN38 ......27 H5
drock Hl BAT TN35 ......27 E4
drock Pk HAS TN34 ......29 H3
dwich Dr STLEO TN38 ......38 B4
dy Cl SLVH TN37 ......28 D3
i Jose Cl RHAS TN35 ......40 C1
nders Cl HAS TN34 ......3 G2
by Rd BEXW TN39 ......43 G2
on Ri BEX TN40 ......44 C2
on Rd RHAS TN35 ......30 D5
on Shore Wy HAS TN34 ......3 K5
'HAS TN35 ......40 D2
'YE TN31 ......5 G1
'SEA TN36 ......15 H4
e Saxons BEXW TN39 * 43 F3
on St SLVH TN37 ......39 E5
onwood Rd BAT TN33 ......8 A5
ool Hl WSEA TN36 ......15 G1
ool Pl BEX TN40 ......45 E1
ool Rd RHAS TN35 ......30 C5
werte Wy HAS TN34 ......2 C7
tes Cl HAS TN34 ......29 H5
bourne Rd BEX TN40 ......36 D5
Rd BEX TN40 ......44 B4
'HAS TN35 ......33 E3
TLEO TN38 ......38 B5
side Rd STLEO TN38 ......38 B5
side Wy STLEO TN38 ......38 B5
view Ter RYE TN31 * 5 E4
ond Av BEX TN40 ......44 D1
gebrook Gdns HAS TN34 ......2 C1
e Sedges STLEO TN38 ......38 A2
gewick Rd BEX TN40 ......36 A5
lescombe Gdns STLEO TN38...38 D1
lescombe Rd North
SLVH TN37 ......28 D4
lescombe Rd South
STLEO TN38 ......38 D2
neston Cl HAS TN34 ......2 B5
lac Gdns HAS TN33 ......18 C1
lac Wy SLVH TN37 ......28 D3
en Acre Cl SLVH TN37 ......28 C3
well Av BEX TN40 ......44 A1
erwater Crs HAS TN34 ......29 F4
pherd's Cl BEXW TN39 ......42 C2
pherd St STLEO TN38 ......39 E5
pherds Wy RHAS TN35 ......32 D4
ppard Pl BAT TN33 * 8 B5
rwood Cl HAS TN34 ......3 F2
ngle Ct STLEO TN38 ......28 A1
pley La BEXW TN39 ......42 D4
lea Vw BAT TN33 ......18 C1
rley Dr SLVH TN37 ......28 D4
Shrublands BEXW TN39 ......43 E3
ey Gn BEXW TN39 ......36 A4
ey Rd BEXW TN39 ......35 H4
hester Rd STLEO TN38 ......39 E4
Cl BEX TN40 ......37 E5
an Rd STLEO TN38 ......28 A5
erhill Av STLEO TN38 ......29 E4
erlands Rd SLVH TN37 ......38 D1
ester Rd BEX TN40 ......44 A1
gleton Wk BEX TN40 ......37 E5
nock Sq HAS TN34 ......3 H5
nner's La BAT TN34 ......24 C1
Slides STLEO TN38 ......28 B5
th Cl BAT TN33 ......24 B3
thy's Cl SLVH TN37 ......29 E3
ugglers Wy RHAS TN35 ......32 D4
th Cliff BEXW TN39 ......43 E4
th Cliff Av BEXW TN39 ......43 E4
thcourt Av BEXW TN39 ......43 F3
thdown Av HAS TN34 ......30 B5
thlands Av BEXW TN39 ......35 G4
thlands Rd BEXW TN39 ......35 G4
th St SLVH TN37 ......39 E4
th Ter HAS TN34 ......2 E4
th Undercliff RYE TN31 ......5 E4
thwater Rd SLVH TN37 ......39 E3
thwood Cl STLEO TN38 ......38 D2
ereign Cl HAS TN34 ......30 A4
Spaldings STLEO TN38 ......38 A2
ckled Wd RHAS TN35 ......30 C5

Spindlewood Dr BEXW TN39......42 C2
The Spinney BEXW TN39 ......18 D2
BEXW TN39 ......42 D3
HAS TN34 ......2 C3
Spray's La BAT TN33 ......20 D1
Springfield Rd STLEO TN38......36 A5
STLEO TN38 ......38 D2
Springfield Vale STLEO TN38...38 D2
Springla STLEO TN38 ......38 D2
Springside Wk STLEO TN38 ......38 B2
Spring St SLVH TN37 ......39 E2
Squirrel Cl BEXW TN39 ......43 E1
Stablefield RHAS TN35 ......21 G1
Stablefields RHAS TN35 * 21 G1
Stable Ms SLVH TN37 * 29 E3
Stanhope Pl STLEO TN38 ......39 E5
Stanier Rd STLEO TN38 ......28 B3
Stanley Rd HAS TN34 ......2 D4
Starrs Cottages HAS TN34 * 3 J5
Starr's Green La BAT TN33 ......18 D2
Starrs Md BAT TN33 ......18 D2
Starwell Cl HAS TN34 ......29 F5
Station Ap BAT TN33 ......18 C2
HAS TN34 ......2 D5
RYE TN31 ......4 D3
SLVH TN37 ......28 D5
Station Rd BAT TN33 ......26 D3
BEX TN40 ......44 A2
WSEA TN36 ......15 C1
Stevens Cl STLEO TN38 ......36 A4
Stevenson Rd STLEO TN38 ......28 D5
Stirling Rd STLEO TN38 ......28 B3
Stock Dl RHAS TN35 ......32 D4
Stockleigh Rd STLEO TN38 ......39 E4
Stocks Meadow BAT TN33 ......24 B3
Stonebeach Ri STLEO TN38 ......28 B1
Stonefield Pl HAS TN34 ......3 F4
Stonefield Rd HAS TN34 ......3 F5
Stonehouse Dr SLVH TN37 ......20 B1
STLEO TN38 ......38 C1
Stonelink Cl SLVH TN37 ......28 B1
Stonestile La RHAS TN35 ......21 G2
Stone St HAS TN34 ......3 F5
Strand RYE TN31 ......4 D4
Strand Hl WSEA TN36 ......15 H3
Strathmore Ct BEX TN40 * 44 C2
Stream La RHAS TN35 ......33 E3
Streamside Cl HAS TN34 ......3 F4
Streetlands BAT TN33 ......10 A1
The Street BAT TN33 ......10 A2
Strong's Pas HAS TN34 ......3 J5
Strood Rd SLVH TN37 ......39 E1
Stubb La RYE TN31 ......12 B1
Sturdee Pl HAS TN34 * 3 H5
Suffolk Rd BEXW TN39 ......36 A4
Summer Hl STLEO TN38 ......38 B1
Summer Hill Rd BEXW TN39 ......35 F5
Sunningdale Cl BEX TN40 ......44 C2
Sunningdale Dr STLEO TN38 ......38 B4
Sussex Cl BEXW TN39 ......43 F1
Sussex Ct BEX TN40 * 44 B2
Sussex Rd STLEO TN38 ......38 C5
Sutherland Av BEXW TN39 ......43 G3
Sutherland Cl BEXW TN39 ......43 G3
Sutton Pl BEX TN40 ......44 C2
The Suttons STLEO TN38 ......38 B1
Swaines Pas HAS TN34 ......3 J5
Swainham La STLEO TN38 ......27 E5
Swallow Bank STLEO TN38 ......38 A1
Swallow Dr BAT TN33 ......18 D1
Swan Av HAS TN34 * 3 H5
Swan Ter HAS TN34 ......3 H5
Swynford Dr STLEO TN38 ......28 B3
Sycamore Cl BEXW TN39 ......42 C2
Sydney Cl STLEO TN38 ......28 D5
Sydney Little Rd STLEO TN38...27 H4

T
Tackleway HAS TN34 ......3 J5
Tall Ash Dr SLVH TN37 ......29 E4
Tanglewood Coppice BEXW TN39...43 E3
Tangmere Cl BEXW TN39 ......43 E3
Tanyard La WSEA TN36 ......15 G2
Taylor Cl STLEO TN38 ......28 A5
Teal Ct STLEO TN38 ......28 A5
Telford Rd SLVH TN37 ......28 D3
Telham Cl HAS TN34 ......30 A3
Telham La BAT TN33 ......18 C4
Tenterden Ri BEXW TN39 ......29 F5
Terminus Av BEXW TN39 ......43 F3
Terminus Rd BEXW TN39 ......43 F3
Terrace Rd SLVH TN37 ......39 E4
Thakeham Cl BEX TN40 ......37 E5
Thanet Wy HAS TN34 ......2 C1

Theaklen Dr STLEO TN38 ......38 D1
Third Av BEX TN40 ......36 D5
Thomas Brassey Cl SLVH TN37...28 D3
Thornbank Crs BEXW TN39 ......43 F3
Thorne Crs BEXW TN39 ......35 G5
The Thorns RHAS TN35 ......23 G5
Ticehurst Cl RHAS TN35 ......30 C5
Tile Barn Rd STLEO TN38 ......28 B4
Tilekiln La RHAS TN35 ......31 E4
Tilgate Dr BEXW TN39 ......42 D3
Tillingham Av RYE TN31 ......4 C4
Tillington Ter RHAS TN35 ......40 C1
Tithe Barn Fld WSEA TN36 ......14 B5
Tiverton Dr BEX TN40 ......44 C1
Tollgates BAT TN33 ......17 H1
Top Cross Rd BEX TN40 ......37 E4
Torfield Cl HAS TN34 ......3 J4
Tower Rd SLVH TN37 ......39 E2
Tower Rd West STLEO TN38 ......38 D3
Towerscroft Av SLVH TN37 ......28 D3
Tower St RYE TN31 ......5 E3
Trafalgar Cl SLVH TN37 ......28 B1
Travellers La RHAS TN35 ......30 C5
Trinity Ms HAS TN34 * 2 D6
Trinity St HAS TN34 ......2 D6
Trinity Vis HAS TN34 ......2 C6
Truman Dr SLVH TN37 ......28 B2
Tudor Av STLEO TN38 ......38 C4
Turkey Rd BEXW TN39 ......34 D4
Turnberry Cl STLEO TN38 ......38 B4
Turner Cl BEX TN40 ......44 B1
Twyford Crs SLVH TN37 ......29 E4
Tyndale Av BEXW TN39 ......42 C1

U
Uckham La BAT TN33 ......8 C4
Udimore Rd RYE TN31 ......4 A5
Undercliff STLEO TN38 ......39 E5
Undercliffe STLEO TN38 * 39 E5
Undercliff Ter STLEO TN38 * 39 E5
Union St SLVH TN37 ......39 E2
Uplands Cl BEXW TN39 ......35 F5
The Uplands STLEO TN38 * 38 D4
Upper Broomgrove Rd
HAS TN34 ......30 B5
Upper Church Rd STLEO TN38...28 D4
Upper Clarence Rd SLVH TN37...39 E2
Upper Glen Rd SLVH TN37 ......28 D5
Upper Lake BAT TN33 ......18 B1
Upper Maze Hl STLEO TN38......38 D3
Upper Park Rd HAS TN34 ......2 A2
SLVH TN37 ......39 E2
Upper Sea Rd BEX TN40 ......44 B2
Upper South Rd SLVH TN37 ......39 E2

V
Vale Rd BAT TN33 ......7 H5
SLVH TN37 ......39 E1
Vale Vw RHAS TN35 * 21 G1
Valley Side Rd RHAS TN35 ......30 C5
Vantage Wk STLEO TN38 ......38 D1
Venture Cl BEX TN40 ......44 D2
Verdant Cl HAS TN34 ......2 B4
Vermont Wy SLVH TN37 ......28 B2
Verulam Pl SLVH TN37 ......2 C7
Vicarage Flats HAS TN34 * 3 H2
Vicarage La RHAS TN35 ......21 F2
Vicarage Rd HAS TN34 ......3 G3
Victoria Av RHAS TN35 ......30 C4
Victoria Ct STLEO TN38 * 38 D5
Victoria Rd BEXW TN39 ......43 H2
View Bank RHAS TN35 ......40 D1
Village Cl BEXW TN39 ......42 C2
Village Ms BEXW TN39 ......42 C2
Villa Rd SLVH TN37 ......2 A7
Vinehall Cl HAS TN34 ......30 A3
Virgin's Cft BAT TN33 ......8 B4
Virgin's La BAT TN33 ......8 B4

W
Wadhurst Cl SLVH TN37 ......28 D3
Wadhurst La BAT TN33 ......7 H4
Wainwright Cl RHAS TN35 ......27 H5
Wainwright Rd BEXW TN39 ......43 H2
Waites La RHAS TN35 ......32 C3
Wakehams Cl BEXW TN39 ......36 A4
Waldegrave St HAS TN34 ......3 F5
Walden Ter BAT TN33 * 18 C1
Walton Cl RHAS TN35 ......29 E3

Walton Pk BEXW TN39 ......43 F2
Wannock Cl BEX TN40 ......37 E5
Ward Wy BEXW TN39 ......35 G5
Warnham Gdns BEXW TN39 ......42 D4
Warren Cl STLEO TN38 ......38 A3
Warren Rd RHAS TN35 ......32 A4
Warrior Gdns SLVH TN37 ......39 E4
Warrior Sq SLVH TN37 ......39 E4
Warrior St SLVH TN37 ......2 A7
Wartling Cl STLEO TN38 ......28 B5
Warwick Rd BEXW TN39 ......43 F1
Washington Av SLVH TN37 ......28 B2
Watchbell La RYE TN31 ......5 E4
Watchbell St RYE TN31 ......5 E4
Watergate BEXW TN39 ......35 H3
Waterloo Cl SLVH TN37 ......28 B1
Watermen's Ct HAS TN34 ......29 C5
Watermill Cl BEXW TN39 ......35 H3
Watermill Dr STLEO TN38 ......27 H5
Watermill La BEXW TN39 ......35 H3
Water Mint Cl STLEO TN38 ......28 A5
Waterside Cl HAS TN34 ......30 B5
Waterworks Cottages
HAS TN34 * 3 F4
Waterworks Rd HAS TN34 ......3 F4
Wattle's Wish BAT TN33 ......8 A4
Waverley Ct SLVH TN37 * 2 C7
Wayside SLVH TN37 * 38 D1
Wealden Wy BEXW TN39 ......34 C5
Welbeck Av STLEO TN38 ......38 D5
Wellesley Cl BEXW TN39 ......42 D3
Wellesley Ct HAS TN34 ......3 G5
Wellington Ms HAS TN34 ......3 F4
Wellington Pl HAS TN34 ......2 E6
Wellington Rd HAS TN34 ......3 G5
Wellington Sq HAS TN34 ......3 F6
Wellington Ter HAS TN34 * 3 F5
Wellis Gdns STLEO TN38 ......38 C3
Welton Ri SLVH TN37 ......28 D2
Wentworth Cl BEX TN40 ......44 D1
Wentworth Wy STLEO TN38......38 B3
West Ascent STLEO TN38 ......38 D5
Westaway Dr BEXW TN39 ......43 E3
Westbrook La RHAS TN35 ......11 C5
Westcourt Dr BEXW TN39 ......43 F3
Westdene Cl SLVH TN37 ......29 E2
West Down Rd BEXW TN39 ......35 G4
Westerleigh Cl STLEO TN38 ......38 C3
Western Rd BEX TN40 ......44 A3
SLVH TN37 ......39 E4
Westfield La SLVH TN37 ......43 E5
Westham Cl BEXW TN39 ......43 E5
West Hill Rd STLEO TN38 ......38 C5
Westminster Crs HAS TN34 ......30 A4
Westmoreland Cl STLEO TN38...28 B5
West Pde BEXW TN39 ......43 H4
West St HAS TN34 ......3 H6
RYE TN31 ......5 E4
West Undercliff RYE TN31 ......4 C4
West Vw HAS TN34 ......3 K1
Westville Rd BEXW TN39 ......43 G2
Whatlington Rd BAT TN33 ......8 C4
Whatlington Wy STLEO TN38...37 H1
Wheatfield Ct SLVH TN37 ......29 E3
Wheel La RHAS TN35 ......21 F2
Whitefriars Rd HAS TN34 ......3 H2
White Hill Av BEXW TN39 ......43 E2
White Hill Dr BEXW TN39 ......43 E2
Whitehouse Av BEXW TN39 ......35 H4
White Rock HAS TN34 ......2 D7
White Rock Gdns HAS TN34 ......2 D6
White Rock Rd HAS TN34 ......2 D7
Whittington's Wy HAS TN34 ......30 B4
Whittlewood Cl STLEO TN38 ......38 A1
Whitworth Rd SLVH TN37 ......28 D1
Whydown Cottages BEXW TN39 *34 C4
Whydown Hl BAT TN33 ......10 A4
Whydown Rd BEXW TN39 ......34 B3
Wickham Av BEXW TN39 ......43 H3
Wickham Rock La WSEA TN36...15 F5
Wilkins Wy BEX TN40 ......36 D5
William Rd STLEO TN38 ......38 A4
Willingdon Av BEXW TN39 ......43 G2
STLEO TN38 ......28 C3
Willingdon Cl STLEO TN38 ......28 C3
Willingdon Wy STLEO TN38 ......28 C3
Willowbed Wk HAS TN34 ......29 G4
Willow Dr BEXW TN39 ......42 C1
Willow End HAS TN34 ......29 H4
The Willows SLVH TN37 ......28 C3
Willow Stream Cl RHAS TN35...23 E2
Wilmington Rd HAS TN34 ......30 A5
Wilton Court Man BEX TN40 * 44 A3
Wilton Rd BEX TN40 ......44 A3
Winceby Cl BEXW TN39 ......43 E4
Winchelsea La RHAS TN35 ......31 E3
Winchelsea Rd RHAS TN35 ......30 D4
RYE TN31 ......4 D4
Winding St HAS TN34 ......3 H5

Windmill Dr *BEXW* TN39..........35 H5
Windmill Rd *STLEO* TN38..........38 D1
Windsor Rd *BEXW* TN39 ....43 H2
  SLVH TN37..........28 D5
Wineham Wy *BEX* TN40..........44 D2
Wingate Cl *STLEO* TN38..........38 C2
Winston Dr *BEXW* TN39 ....43 E2
Winterbourne Cl *HAS* TN34 ....2 C4
Wishing Tree Cl *STLEO* TN38..........38 B1
Wishing Tree La *STLEO* TN38..........38 B1
Wishing Tree Rd *STLEO* TN38..........38 B1
Wishing Tree Rd North
  STLEO TN38..........38 C4

Wish Ward *RYE* TN31..........4 D4
Withyham Rd *BEXW* TN39..........42 C4
Wittersham Ri *STLEO* TN38..........38 A1
Wode Rd *BAT* TN33..........24 A5
Woodbrook Rd *HAS* TN34..........29 H5
Woodcombe *HAS* TN34..........29 H4
Woodhams Cl *BAT* TN33..........18 B1
Woodland Ri *BAT* TN40..........44 C2
The Woodlands *HAS* TN34..........29 C5
Woodlands Wy *HAS* TN34..........29 G2
Woodland Vale Rd *SLVH* TN37..........39 E3
Woodland Wy *BAT* TN33..........26 D4
  RHAS TN35..........32 C3

Woodsgate Av *BEXW* TN39 ....36 A5
Woodsgate Pk *BEXW* TN39 ....35 G5
Woods Pas *HAS* TN34..........3 K5
Woodspring Cl *SLVH* TN37..........28 D3
Woodstock Rd *BEXW* TN39..........34 C5
Woodville Rd *BEXW* TN39..........43 H3
Workhouse La *RHAS* TN35..........21 G1
  WSEA TN36..........14 B5
Worsham La *BEX* TN40..........36 D4
Wren Ct *BAT* TN33..........18 D1
  STLEO TN38 *..........28 A5
Wrestwood Cl *BEX* TN40..........36 B5
Wrestwood Rd *BEX* TN40.:..........36 B5

Wrotham Cl *HAS* TN34..........29
Wychurst Gdns *BEX* TN40..........36
Wykeham Rd *HAS* TN34..........2

Y

Yew Tree Cl *HAS* TN34..........29
York Buildings *HAS* TN34 *..........2
York Gdns *HAS* TN34..........2
York Rd *BEX* TN40..........45
  SLVH TN37..........39

Index - featured places

1066 Battle of Hastings
  Abbey & Battlefield
  BAT TN33 ....18 B1
1066 Story in Hastings Castle
  HAS TN34 ....3 G5
All Saints CE Junior School
  RHAS TN35 ....40 C2
All Saints CE Primary School
  BEXW TN39 ....35 H4
Amberley School
  BEX TN40 ....44 A1
Amusement Centre *BEX* TN40 .....44 A4
Arthur Blackman Clinic
  SLVH TN37 ....28 D4
Battle Abbey Preparatory
  School *BEX* TN40 ....44 C1
Battle Abbey School *BAT* TN33 ..18 B1
Battle & Langton CE Primary
  School *BAT* TN33 ....18 A1
Battle Museum of Local
  History *BAT* TN33 ....18 B1
Beauport Park Hotel
  SLVH TN37 ....20 B5
Beeching Park Industrial Estate
  BEXW TN39 ....43 H2
Bexhill Amateur Athletic Club
  BEXW TN39 ....43 H2
Bexhill Cemetery *BEXW* TN39 ....35 E3
Bexhill College *BEXW* TN39 ....35 G4
Bexhill High School Technology
  College *BEXW* TN39 ....43 H1
Bexhill Hospital *BEX* TN40 ....36 K5
Bexhill Leisure Centre
  BEXW TN39 ....43 H1
Bexhill Sailing Club *BEX* TN40 ......44 B3
Bexhill Squash Rackets Club
  BEX TN40 ....44 C2
Boltons Clinic *STLEO* TN38 ....38 D2
Brakes Coppice Park *BAT* TN33 ....27 E1
Brickwall Hotel *BAT* TN33 ....10 A1
Buchanan Hospital
  STLEO TN38 ....38 D2
Buckswood School *RHAS* TN35 ....23 G2
Cambridge Gardens College
  HAS TN34 ....2 D6
Castledown CPN School
  HAS TN34 ....3 H2
Catsfield CE Primary School
  BAT TN33 ....17 F5
Charters Ancaster College
  BEXW TN39 ....35 G5
Charters Ancaster School
  BEX TN40 ....44 D1
Chatsworth Hotel *HAS* TN34 ....2 D7
Churchills Industrial Estate
  STLEO TN38 ....27 H4
Churchwood Primary School
  STLEO TN38 ....28 B5
Claremont School *SLVH* TN37 ....20 D4
Claverham Community College
  BAT TN33 ....17 G1
Cloudesley Shovell House
  HAS TN34 ....3 J5
Community Centre *BEX* TN40 .....44 B1
Community Education Centre &
  Library *RYE* TN31 ....5 E4
Conqueror Industrial Estate
  STLEO TN38 ....28 B2
Conquest Hospital *SLVH* TN37 ....29 F2
Cooden Beach Golf Club
  BEXW TN39 ....42 B4

Crowhurst CE Primary School
  BAT TN33 ....26 D3
Curzon Picture Playhouse
  Cinema *BEXW* TN39 ....44 A2
De La Warr Pavilion
  BEXW TN39 ....44 A3
De Luxe Leisure Centre
  HAS TN34 ....3 G6
Dudley Infant School
  RHAS TN35 ....40 C2
East Hill Cliff Lift *HAS* TN34 ....3 J5
EF International School of
  English
  SLVH TN37 ....2 A6
Elphinstone Community School
  HAS TN34 ....40 A1
Eversfield Hospital
  STLEO TN38 ....38 C5
Falaise Hall *HAS* TN34 ....2 C6
Filsham Valley School
  STLEO TN38 ....38 A4
Fisheries Museum *HAS* TN34 ....3 J6
Flower Makers Museum
  HAS TN34 ....3 G5
The Freda Gardham Community
  School *RYE* TN31 ....5 F3
Glyne Gap Special School
  BEX TN40 ....45 E1
The Grove School *STLEO* TN38 ...38 B2
Guestling Bradshaw CE
  Primary School *RHAS* TN35 .....23 G5
Hasting Medical Centre
  HAS TN34 ....2 E5
Hastings Cemetery *HAS* TN34 ....30 B3
Hastings College of Arts
  &Technology *STLEO* TN38 .....38 D5
Hastings Country Park
  RHAS TN35 ....31 H5
Hastings Crematorium
  HAS TN34 ....30 A3
Hastings Education College
  STLEO TN38 ....38 B4
Hastings Indoor Market
  HAS TN34 ....3 F6
Hastings Museum & Art Gallery
  HAS TN34 ....2 C5
Hastings Pier *HAS* TN34 ....39 G5
Hastings & St Leonards
  Sailing Club *STLEO* TN38 .....38 D5
Hastings Town FC *HAS* TN34 .....30 A5
Helenswood Upper School
  HAS TN34 ....30 A4
Heritage Centre & Town Model
  RYE TN31 ....4 D4
High Beech Hotel *SLVH* TN37 .....28 B2
Highfield Business Park
  STLEO TN38 ....27 H4
Highwoods Golf Club
  BEXW TN39 ....35 E4
Hillcrest School *RHAS* TN35 .....31 E3
The Hope Anchor Hotel
  RYE TN31 ....4 D4
Icklesham Primary School
  WSEA TN36 ....14 A4
Jempsons Trading Estate
  RYE TN31 ....4 D4
King Offa Primary School
  BEXW TN39 ....43 G1
Lamb House (NT) *RYE* TN31 .....5 E4
Landgate Arch *RYE* TN31 ....5 E3
Lifeboat Station *HAS* TN34 ....3 H6

Little Common Primary School
  BEXW TN39 ....42 D2
Little Ridge CP School
  SLVH TN37 ....29 E3
Little Ridge Surgery
  SLVH TN37 ....29 E3
Megabowl *BEX* TN40 ....45 E2
Mercateria Business Centre
  STLEO TN38 ....39 E5
Mermaid Inn Hotel *RYE* TN31 ....4 D4
The Mews Business Centre
  BEX TN40 ....44 A2
Mount Pleasant Hospital
  SLVH TN37 ....28 C4
Museum of Costumes
  and Bygones
  BEX TN40 ....44 B2
Net Shops *HAS* TN34 ....3 J6
New Horizons School
  STLEO TN38 ....28 B3
Ninfield CE Primary School
  BAT TN33 ....24 B3
Odeon Cinema
  HAS TN34 ....2 E6
Old Town Hall Museum of Local
  History *HAS* TN34 ....3 H5
Ore Business Park *RHAS* TN35 ....40 B1
Pebsham Community Primary
  School *BEX* TN40 ....45 E1
Powder Mills Hotel *BAT* TN33 ..18 A3
Premier Travel Inn *SLVH* TN37 ...28 C2
Priory Meadow Shopping
  Centre *HAS* TN34 ....2 E5
Ravenside Retail & Leisure Park
  BEX TN40 ....45 E2
Red Lake CP School
  RHAS TN35 ....30 D4
Robsack Wood Community
  School *STLEO* TN38 ....38 A1
Rockys Leisure Centre
  HAS TN34 ....2 D7
Rope Walk Shopping Centre
  RYE TN31 ....4 D4
The Rother Ironworks *RYE* TN31 ..5 E4
Royal Victoria Hotel
  STLEO TN38 ....38 D5
Rutherfords Business Park
  BAT TN33 ....9 F3
Rye Castle Museum *RYE* TN31 ....5 E4
Rye Community Clinic
  RYE TN31 ....4 D3
Rye Football & CC *RYE* TN31 ......5 E3
Rye Industrial Estate *RYE* TN31 ...5 F5
Rye Lodge Hotel *RYE* TN31 ....5 E4
Rye Sports Centre *RYE* TN31 ......4 D3
St Andrews Market *HAS* TN34 ....3 F5
St Leonards CE Primary School
  STLEO TN38 ....38 C4
St Leonards FC *HAS* TN34 ....30 A4
St Mary Magdalen Primary
  School *BEX* TN40 ....36 D5
St Marys School *BEX* TN40 ....36 C5
St Mary Star of the Sea RC
  Primary School *SLVH* TN37 ....2 A5
St Pauls CE Primary School
  SLVH TN37 ....2 A3
St Peter & St Paul CE Primary
  School *BEX* TN40 ....44 A2
St Richards Catholic College
  BEX TN40 ....44 C2
St Vincent School *STLEO* TN38 ....38 B5

Sandown Primary School
  HAS TN34 30
Saxon Mount Special School
  STLEO TN38 38
Sealife Aquarium *HAS* TN34 3
Sea Road Surgery *BEX* TN40 44
Sedlescombe CE School
  BAT TN33 10
Sedlescombe Golf Club
  BAT TN33 10
Shearbarn Holiday Park
  RHAS TN35 40
Shipwreck Heritage Centre
  HAS TN34 3
Sidley Primary School
  BEX TN40 36
Sidley Sports Club *BEXW* TN39 36
Silverdale Primary School
  SLVH TN37 28
Smugglers Adventure *HAS* TN34 ...3
The Stables Theatre *HAS* TN34 3
Summerfield Leisure Centre
  HAS TN34 2
Summerfields Business Centre
  HAS TN34 2
Sussex Private Clinic
  STLEO TN38 38
TEN66 Golf Club *SLVH* TN37 20
Thomas Peacocke Community
  College *RYE* TN31 4
Tilling Green Infant School
  RYE TN31 4
Torfield Special School
  HAS TN34 3
Travelodge *HAS* TN34 2
Venture Industrial Park
  STLEO TN38 38
War Memorial *BEX* TN40 44
Warrior Square Surgery
  SLVH TN37 39
Wellington Square Medical
  Centre *HAS* TN34 3
Westerleigh St Leonards School
  STLEO TN38 38
Westerleigh School
  STLEO TN38 38
Westfield Primary School
  RHAS TN35 21
West Hill Cliff Lift *HAS* TN34 3
West Hill Community Centre
  HAS TN34 3
West St Leonards CP School
  STLEO TN38 38
Wheel Park Farm Industrial
  Estate *RHAS* TN35 21
White Rock Theatre
  HAS TN34 2
William Parker Community
  Athletics Arena *HAS* TN34 29
William Parker School
  HAS TN34 3
Winchelsea Court Hall Museum
  WSEA TN36 15
Winchelsea St Thomas CE
  Primary School *WSEA* TN36 15
Yesterday's World *BAT* TN33 18
Young People's Hall &
  Salvation Army *HAS* TN34 2
Ypres Tower *RYE* TN31 5

Acknowledgements

Schools address data provided by Education Direct.

Petrol station information supplied by Johnsons

One-way street data provided by © Tele Atlas N.V. Tele Atlas

Garden centre information provided by

Garden Centre Association  Britains best garden centres

Wyevale Garden Centres

The statement on the front cover of this atlas is sourced,
selected and quoted from a reader comment and
feedback form received in 2004